PRAISE FOR *THE WAY UP*

Moving up the corporate ladder doesn't naturally occur by just being yourself. You need to learn the way up, and this book provides pragmatic advice that will help you greatly, especially if you are a professional of color. Act today!

— Jihoon Rim, NYU Stern Visiting Professor and former CEO of Kakao

Dr. Errol Pierre has provided a pathway to minority inclusion in the highest levels of corporate America by sharing his enthralling personal story. An important read for those pursuing leadership roles and aspiring to the C-suite.

— Shelly McDonald-Pinkett, MD, FACP, CPHQ, Chair (I) Department of Medicine, Howard University College of Medicine

Executives of color in corporate settings face unique challenges that require intention, support, and specific strategies to facilitate success. The stories and truths shared in Errol's book provide very useful insights and examples that can help any professional reach their goals and navigate increasingly complex realities in the workplace...I highly recommend it!

— Willem Genece, Executive Advisor, Coach and Coaching Practice Leader at Crenshaw Associates

Errol Pierre's career, with still many years to go, has already been highly successful. As someone who "knew him when," I am not surprised. Errol possessed both a high IQ and a strong bias for hard work, even as a recent college graduate. He held himself to a high standard of performance and simultaneously was someone everyone wanted to work with. I am so thrilled that he is sharing his professional philosophy for achievement and his invaluable lessons learned. This book offers much for everyone.

— Jefferson Grahling, President, Circulo Health

This book should be the rule and guide for any executive of color who is trying to take their career to the next level.

— **Leonard Achan RN, MA, ANP**

The Way Up is a great primer on corporate innovation and change. Errol writes an inspiring book that stands out as a signal of systemic change.

— **Jerrold Delaine, Professor and Real Estate Developer**

THE
WAY
UP

ERROL L. PIERRE
WITH JIM JERMANOK

THE
WAY
UP

CLIMBING THE
CORPORATE MOUNTAIN AS
A PROFESSIONAL OF COLOR

WILEY

Library of Congress Cataloging-in-Publication Data:

Names: Pierre, Errol L., author.
Title: The way up : climbing the corporate mountain as a professional of color / Errol L. Pierre.
Description: Hoboken, New Jersey : John Wiley & Sons, Inc., [2023] |
    Includes bibliographical references and index.
Identifiers: LCCN 2022030909 (print) | LCCN 2022030910 (ebook) | ISBN
    9781119893264 (cloth) | ISBN 9781119893288 (adobe pdf) | ISBN
    9781119893271 (epub)
Subjects: LCSH: African Americans—Employment. | Career development—United
    States. | Office politics—United States. | Management—United States.
Classification: LCC HD8081.A65 P54 2023 (print) | LCC HD8081.A65 (ebook)
    | DDC 331.6/396073—dc23/eng/20220805
LC record available at https://lccn.loc.gov/2022030909
LC ebook record available at https://lccn.loc.gov/2022030910

Cover Design and Image: Wiley
SKY10037301_102522

CONTENTS

PREFACE

Since the COVID-19 pandemic began, the world has been presented with a plethora of lessons on diversity, equity, and inclusion (DE&I), with racial equity surging to the top of many corporate conversations. Leaders, corporations, and organizations were forced to reevaluate strategies to infuse diversity, equality, and inclusion into their organizational cultures and value sets. Society demanded an honest assessment to wipe out structural inequalities that limit the career trajectories of employees of color.

The simple reality for many corporations is that cultivating an environment where all employees are able to progress equitably requires systemic change. However, such change has been severely lacking to date and unsupported by a genuine commitment to making it happen, despite the creation of numerous new diversity programs.

The deaths of George Floyd, Breonna Taylor, Ahmaud Arbery, Rayshard Brooks, and so many other Black Americans has brought the long history of systemic racism in the United States into sharp focus. Pressure is growing on corporate leaders to consider how their companies can address and correct ongoing racial injustices. However, they have encountered such pressures in the past and have essentially chosen to do very little. *Is it realistic for us to expect substantial change now?*

Add to this the fact that the lives and livelihoods of people of color (POC) in America have been disproportionately affected by the current pandemic. Both Black and Hispanic/Latinx Americans have died from COVID-19 at more than twice the rate of White Americans. Those who survived were much more likely to have been fired or furloughed. These bitter realities further emphasize the need for serious change in corporate America.

Corporate America's top ranks look nothing like the country they serve. We must consider the daunting statistics for a moment. Black Americans make up 12.4% of our country's population.[1] But they only represent 8% of white-collar professionals, a number that has stayed steady since 2013.[2] This despite an increasing number of Black graduates from colleges and universities. Furthermore, Black professionals in 2018 held just 3.3% of all executive or senior leadership roles, which are defined as within two reporting levels of the CEO, according to the U.S. Equal Employment Opportunity Commission.[3] This number has also remained static for decades and has been justified and condoned by corporate leaders who insist that there are simply not enough qualified candidates—a patently false claim.

Among Fortune 500 companies in America, less than 1% of CEOs are Black![4] Today, there are only four, down from a high of six in 2012 according to *Forbes*.[5] For Black women, the situation is even bleaker. In 2020, women held the top job at just 37 of these 500 companies, a record high of 7.4%.[6] However, only one of these women is Black. Numbers improve only slightly for Hispanic/Latinx CEOs, representing 4% of the Fortune 500, despite representing 18.7% of the U.S. population as of the latest census data.[7]

The underrepresentation of Black and Hispanic/Latinx professionals is particularly dire in the highest echelon of corporate America: Boards of Directors. According to *Harvard Business Review*, Black board members represented only 4.1% of the board members accounted for by the Russell 3000—while 37% of these firms did not have any Black board members at all![8] Board members of color represented only 10.4% of all board members pre-pandemic.[9] However, changes have begun to emerge since America's racial awakening. As of 2021, nearly half of all new S&P 500 board members were people of color.[10] While the gains have helped close the gap minimally, certain groups, like Hispanic/Latinx populations still lag far behind.[11] Thus, these changes must become a movement, long-lasting and systemic, as opposed to a mere moment of window dressing or, even worse, tokenism.

Today's workforce contains many millions of deserving and promotable employees of color who are unfairly stuck in lower and mid-level management positions. This population is the target audience and foundation for *The Way Up*, an advisory, anecdotal, and motivational book written for those who seek to attain the executive ranks. This guidebook is a step-by-step approach to understanding the skills and strategies required to elevate oneself in their company or organization. It is told in an easily digestible series of anecdotes that lead to actionable advice. Now more than ever, it is essential for employees of color to learn how to navigate through the halls and digital Zoom calls of corporate America.

In the past, preparation, guidance, and mentorship for diverse candidates was never a true focus area for corporations. Although work was supposedly done in this arena, it was perfunctory at best and such activities never yielded meaningful changes. Once again, the number of underrepresented race and ethnicities in senior-level or C-Suite roles has systemically remained low despite an enormous number of qualified, educated, and experienced candidates.

According to *USA Today*, "For decades, corporate America has failed to hire, promote, and fairly pay Black men and women, stalling many from rising above middle management . . . This stark racial divide has a cascading effect, stagnating income levels and helping to worsen the race, class and wealth gap that is yawning even wider during the COVID-19 pandemic."[12] Until corporate America gets its act together, employees of color need to strategize about how to advance in a system where they are often destined to fail.

I have written *The Way Up* to address these current realities in a meaningful, actionable, and impactful way. In the past 18 years, I was indeed fortunate to find the way up the corporate mountain to a corner office. I am a former chief operating officer of a large health plan and currently serve as senior vice president of the largest nonprofit health plan in New York State. As a frequent speaker and panelist, an alumnus of both Fordham University and New York University, and an active LinkedIn user, I encounter hundreds of Black and Hispanic/Latino employees in middle management who feel stuck in their careers. There's nothing I enjoy more than counseling these aspiring employees on key career decisions. I want to use my story to galvanize and inspire those millions of diverse employees who have managed to make it to white-collar management, but find themselves frustrated on their path to becoming executives.

While corporate leaders say they are seeking to increase their diversity, equity, and inclusion in this day and age, way too many employees of color can no longer tolerate years of stagnant professional growth. The BIPOC (Black, Indigenous, and People of Color) workforce has repeatedly been marginalized, demotivated, and disempowered.

However, there is now a ray of hope. In the past year, an increasing number of American corporate executives have become enlightened to the bleak reality of systemic racism. It is high time for employees of color to be prepared for the opportunities that may present themselves in this new normal, *post-George Floyd world*.

The Way Up incorporates all the life-transforming and career-transforming lessons I have learned throughout the years as well as specific quotes from successful executives of color who also moved up in corporate America. Each chapter of the book provides pragmatic, action-oriented advice for the reader to pursue. The culmination of this advice will yield a full-fledged roadmap for organizational advancement supported by proven strategies, innovative insights, and practical know-how. *The Way Up* will also fill a glaring lapse in available literature on this subject: there are hardly any books advising people of color how to attain senior leadership positions in their companies despite the recent spotlight on diversity, inclusion, and racial equity.

Please note: For purposes of this book, I will use racial and ethnic identity definitions as described in Section 5.7 of the *APA Publication Manual*, Seventh Edition, with full understanding that these terms continue to evolve and be discussed and debated in our society.[13]

INTRODUCTION: THE CORPORATE MOUNTAIN

Yesterday I was clever, so I wanted to change the world. Today I am wise, so I am changing myself.
—Rumi, thirteenth-century Persian poet and Islamic scholar

In 2016, I took my first solo trip to Thailand, with a goal to climb the great Doi Inthanon. Located in the city of Chiang Mai, it is the highest mountain in the entire country. Indeed, it stands at 8,415 feet high. At the top is a shrine called the Summit of Doi Inthanon, a tribute to Inthawichayanon, who was the King Ruler of the second-biggest city in Thailand, Chiang Mai, from 1870 to 1897. Before dying, he requested his ashes be buried there to call attention to the preservation of the forest and wildlife. Since then, Doi Inthanon has been maintained by the Thai government and has become a popular tourist attraction.

Trekking up that mountain takes a lot of logistics and preparation. While there are many trails to the top, it's essential to have a tour guide who will know which trails to explore. For example, the trails Kew Mae Pan or Angka are fairly stable and predictable. However, there are other trails that have not been maintained well at all. They are not only difficult but may be downright dangerous. My tour guide not only helped me navigate which path to take, but also shared other insightful information.

The Thai mountain Doi Inthanon is prone to a variety of unpredictable weather conditions. Whether you hike during the hot dry season or in the rainy season, the weather when you start hiking may be dramatically different when you summit this climate changing mountain at the hike's end. Even though the day started out fairly warm without a cloud in the sky, I was advised by my tour guide to pack a poncho and long sleeves just in case.

On my way, I was mesmerized by the Wachirathan Waterfall, one of many stunning views to absorb on my way to the top. Often, the trails there are winding and circular—certainly not a straight path as you hike up the hills and valleys. While hiking a mountain, it's important to have key supplies on hand. Water and protein bars keep you hydrated and fortified. Other vital equipment should include a walking stick, appropriate climbing boots, bug spray, Band-Aids, sun block—not to mention a map and a compass, which have saved many a climber.

What does this have to do with corporate America? For many people of color, climbing the ranks is more akin to a mountain than a ladder. Ladders have rungs that are equally spread apart, allowing for a measured ascent. Mountains are completely different. Mountain climbing routes are winding and unpredictable. They are root-littered and rock-studded. At times, they require a climber to take a more circular route or to double back if necessary for proper ascent.

However, we don't approach corporate America in that manner. We're not prepared for the trip. We don't have the stamina or the energy for the climb. We haven't packed the necessary tools, equipment, and provisions, nor have we found ourselves an appropriate guide. We fail to realize that the path to the top is not a straight line, but a winding one that will include peaks and valleys. And once we reach a new echelon along our journey, we often don't pause to enjoy the views.

As people of color, we often incorrectly compare ourselves to our White colleagues and their accompanying promotions and raises. The reality is that we're not climbing up the same structure! The corporate ladder exists for some in America, but not for people of color and immigrants. For us, ascending the ranks in corporate America is more akin to climbing a mountain. We're also not prepared for lateral moves along our career. Climbing mountains sometimes requires that we go left or right instead of straight up. Lateral moves in corporate America are sometimes frowned on, but they are almost a necessity for people of color. We must learn to incorporate that level of forethought in our decisions. I learned that walking up a mountain in a circular way can seem slower, but it is safer and wiser, and surely recommended by most guides.

In the same way, we often fail to pack the necessary climbing equipment. For example, we jump into conversations with our boss on our annual performance reviews without the necessary preparation. That is not the time to ask for a raise or a promotion. Those conversations should have taken place well before such a review. Additionally, we underestimate the climb and don't realize the amount of blood, sweat, and tears it will take to reach the top. Some of us may burn out. Many of us exert too much energy early in the climb and can't last the whole way through. We may forget or lose our poncho or compass. When stress or anxiety overcomes us, we're simply not ready for a downpour.

We don't realize how much time we'll spend working on projects that are probably more difficult than those of our White peers—and without the kind of support that they have access to. Through it all, you'll encounter people who won't just seek your downfall along the way—they'll also try to distract you from your mission or vision.

The sooner we realize that our paths for advancing our careers are wildly different from those of our peers, the better we can prepare for our journey. If we can anticipate the highs and lows, the long trails, the detours, and the inclement weather, then we can better prepare for becoming a trailblazer.

Arming employees of color with the right stories, advice, and tools is essential for their growth. Indeed, there are shining examples of top echelon corporate mountain climbers for them to be inspired by. Furthermore, many of the most popular self-help books on career advancement or leadership are written by authors who never made the climb themselves. They're based on stories from those who climbed only corporate ladders, not corporate mountains. No wonder people of color are so underrepresented in the executive corporate ranks.

We must discuss and define success. Success can mean many things to many different people. The journey to the upper echelons of corporate America is just one avenue of fulfillment. But this journey is not for the faint of heart or for those who are unwilling to do the hard work required. However, if the work, warnings, and difficult journey ahead do not deter you, then this book is for you.

CHAPTER 1

Find Your Purpose and Your Passion

The Resignation Letter That Led Me Back to My Truth

Man. He sacrifices his health in order to make money. Then he sacrifices money to recuperate his health. And then he is so anxious about the future that he does not enjoy the present or the future; he lives as if he is never going to die, and then dies having never really lived.

—*His Holiness the 14th Dalai Lama of Tibet*

I've written three resignation letters in my 18-year career, and I've had the somewhat unusual experience of working at only two companies so far in my entire professional career. I left my first organization after close to 10 years, and then returned to it after about 6 years at a second company. Typing my third resignation letter was the result of one of the most difficult decisions I ever made. I remember my trembling hand when I was composing the letter in Microsoft Word. By this point, I had reached the pinnacle of my career. I was a Black executive in a C-Suite role; an anomaly. My social capital had instantly exploded. I was invited to speak on numerous panels to share my secrets of success. An investment bank asked me to join a panel of distinguished professionals to discuss the psychology of being Black in corporate America. I was even invited to a rooftop brunch one summer with Black celebrities to hang out, network, and mingle. This new world I was introduced to came about because of my new executive title. A new C-Suite title that had the benefit of opening doors that were previously closed. Doors I never even knew about. Yet here I was, resigning from the job that had brought me so much prestige and cachet.

At the time of writing my letter, I was depressed. My brain told me I should be happy because the world said I was a success, but my heart felt unfulfilled and defeated. I had an empty feeling inside of my soul that yearned for purpose. It is unsettling to strive for something your whole life and, upon achieving it, not experience the jubilation you expected. For so many years, I idolized the three letters "COO." They were my oasis. If I could just achieve a certain executive level in corporate America, I thought would be happy. I believed I would finally be content.... How wrong I was.

In the height of my feelings of emptiness, I remember waking up at 5 a.m. to start my daily commute to work. I soon arrived in downtown Manhattan blocks away from my office. If I did not have a meeting or conference call scheduled, I would walk around the South Street Seaport aimlessly. At the time, there seemed to be an invisible line from the entrance of my office building. Any time I passed through that entryway, I would automatically feel a heavy sadness weigh upon my shoulders. I wondered why.

Could it be that I had meticulously planned for this role for the past 10 years and miscalculated the benefits? To be clear, that time consisted of 120 months of intentionally making professional and personal decisions that would uniquely qualify me to reach the top. I chose the jobs to apply for specifically patterned on how previous successful executives reached their C-Suite roles. Based on promotional advice from various leaders in my company, I went back to school for a graduate degree specializing in health policy and financial management. I focused on volunteering and community service because I felt it was important, although I did benefit indirectly from the networking opportunities that soon revealed themselves.

Everything I did had a rhyme and reason. The journey was long but I never let up. I was never deterred or discouraged. The culmination of all my hard work and focus led me to this new position. My new reality. But what happens to the dog chasing the car when that car finally stops? What's next, if anything? Not knowing my next steps left me with feelings of emptiness.

Stanley E. Grayson

Board Member of TD Bank, N.A., and Mutual of America Investment Corporation

"I grew up in a household where if I heard this once, I probably heard it a thousand times: just being as good is not enough, you have to be better. And every day I hear that little voice . . . whether it was in business or sports, I always found that the harder I work the luckier I got."

I placed too much emphasis on my new position. I learned that external validation can be fleeting and superficial. It only goes so far in feeling accomplished and fulfilled from within. Although I was earning more money than ever before, I discovered that the formula for enhancing my income literally equated to the suffering of others. If I cut my operating budget, for example, I earned a higher bonus. But such a budget cut meant layoffs and even more. A husband or wife coming home from work that day and telling their family that they were out of work. It seemed that the more layoffs I approved, the more money I would earn. In good conscience, I could not do it. I could not send parents home without an income. I would not do it!

These types of strategies are commonplace in corporate America. Being in my position led me to hurt, not help, my community. I knew that if I was not part of the solution, then I was becoming a part of the problem. At the time, I knew my talents were not being used for the improvement of my neighborhood. The Bronx is the bottom of the barrel in healthcare. It is the 62nd county out of 62 in New York state when it comes to health outcomes. How could I squander God's gifts and blessings by not helping those less fortunate than I was? Especially those who reminded me of my own parents: working class immigrants just trying to make ends meet. My dad found the way out from *the farm to the fast city*. His homeland, Haiti, is the poorest country in the Western Hemisphere. He grew up on a small farm and ended up with a son working in a corporate corner office. I felt compelled to not only never forget *where* I came from and *whom* I came from, but also to make damn sure I helped as many people as I possibly could along the way.

So, with a quivering hand, I finished that resignation letter, printed it out, and personally handed it to my CEO. I walked back to my desk waiting for the consequences of my decision, but my head was held high.

LESSON 1.1: PRIORITIZE YOUR PURPOSE

Before you start out your career journey, keep the end in mind. If you have already started your career, it is still not too late to define your purpose. Your purpose becomes your compass as you march up your corporate mountain. Your purpose will guide you on where to go. Your purpose will tell you when to say "yes" to a particular opportunity, but most importantly will also help you learn to say "no" to certain opportunities as well. Your purpose is the reason you are on the planet. Take the time to ask yourself why you are here. If you start there, the rest of your life will quickly fall into place. And rest assured, your purpose may change over time, and that is completely okay.

I left a role I spent 15 years pursuing because I placed a fancy title and a higher salary ahead of my purpose. When you compromise your purpose on your way to the top, you'll inevitably wake up one day with everything you ever asked for, but still feel empty inside. For the sake of your career and your mental health, you need to always make sure you are a part of something bigger than yourself.

In my experience, I've seen that many people, out of expedience, first pursue a job, and then try to transform it into a career. They then attempt to retrofit that career into their purpose. Do not work backwards. Pursuing your life this way can lead you to trying to fit square pegs into round holes. Your purpose always must come first! Through mentoring, I learned my place on Earth is to be a resource to others on their path to becoming the best version of themselves. My job in advancing health equity has become the vehicle I use to pursue my purpose.

Once you understand your purpose on Earth, other life decisions become easy. Every job I have taken and excelled in has brought me closer to my purpose. Once you have purpose, you do not have to worry about your salary. You'll be getting paid for work you would have done for free. Work that aligns with your passions. You'll find that the benefits of working will greatly outweigh any of the negatives, costs, or burdens. With purpose, you never feel lost.

There are too many rudderless employees unhappy in their career. I speak with them often. Their unhappiness largely starts with a misalignment between their profession and their purpose. Their position in the company does not allow them to pursue their passions. They prioritize their paycheck above and beyond all other pursuits.

The other advantage of living out your purpose is if you ever do end up in a job that does not align with your mind, body, and soul, you will know very quickly. Your spirit will scream it from the rafters. While reaching the pinnacle of my professional career in title, salary, and responsibilities was an amazing achievement, it did not align with my purpose. That's where the emptiness came from. If you are only working for a title and a higher salary, you will always long for more. Money cannot buy enough things to fill the emptiness you will feel in your heart.

LESSON 1.2: LINK YOUR PASSION TO YOUR PROFESSION

Once you've landed on a purpose, you can start to link your passion to your profession—to be a part of something bigger than yourself.

Before there were Harpo Productions and OWN (the Oprah Winfrey Network), there was a little Black girl named Oprah who used to interview her dolls.

Before becoming a regular on *Shark Tank*, as a young man Daymond John sewed wool hats and sold them on his block.

Before she led Pacific Gas and Electric as the first Latina CEO of a Fortune 500 company, Geisha Williams worked a summer job at a local power company and discovered her passion.

What these powerful people of color were able to do was turn a tiny seed of passion into gigantic redwoods of prosperity. They all became part of something bigger than themselves. They were motivated and led by their passion.

Finding a project to pour yourself into may seem daunting. I've learned to lean on the circumstances that are hidden right in front of you. For example, my love for mentoring came from the pain of not really having an older brother involved in my life. With a 10-year age gap between us, my older brother and I were never really close. As I grew up, I always longed for a better relationship with him. In his absence, I subconsciously gravitated toward older students in both high school and college. For example, while running track and field as a freshman in college, I befriended Robert Westman, a recent Fordham graduate who was the captain of the track and field team. He would later be inducted into the Fordham University Hall of Fame. I looked up to him, and we formed a close bond. He took me under his wing and became a brother to me during my first few years of college. He helped me keep my head on straight. Older male figures like Robert helped fill the vacuum I felt from not having a meaningful relationship with my older brother. As I got older, I felt compelled to do the same for others and pay it forward.

Many of our passions originate from painful passages of our life. Take the time to reflect on those types of life experiences and write them down. Your results will become the basis for any of your future decisions. Whenever you pursue a new endeavor, the key question to ask is if it brings you closer to your passion. If the answer is yes, move forward and pursue. If it is no, reverse course and reevaluate.

In economics, there is a concept called *opportunity cost*. The idea behind opportunity cost is to quantify the value of the choice you decide against. For example, choosing to go back to school means that, to you, the value of school is higher than whatever you decided *not* to do.

Life will always be about decisions and tradeoffs. Understanding the opportunity costs of your decisions through the lens of your passion is the best way to ensure that you stay fulfilled in all that you do. Any time you make a decision that does not align with your purpose and passion, you are placing less value on the very reason why you are on this planet. It makes no sense to compromise your purpose.

LESSON 1.3: THINK BIGGER THAN YOURSELF

Take a minute to realize that, whatever obstacles you are facing in life, you're probably not alone. As you brainstorm solutions to those problems, always remember to think bigger than yourself. The absence of my older brother turned into a lifelong commitment to mentoring young men of color in New York City. Similarly, try to solve your own problems by coming up with solutions that will benefit the rest of your community. Once you view the world through this lens, doors of opportunity will open up for you. In an attempt to fix the bigger issue, you will meet other people along the way who will want to help. You will slowly build a coalition of the willing. If you were bad at math as a kid, volunteer at an afterschool math-tutoring program. Who knows, you may even start your own tutoring company. The possibilities are endless. Dream audaciously.

CHAPTER 2

Embrace Your Defining Moments
A Bright Future Is Only Built Upon the Foundations of Your Past

Un pour tous, tous pour un.
(All for one and one for all.)
—*Alexandre Dumas, in his legendary 1844 novel*
The Three Musketeers

My father, Stuart Pierre, emigrated from Haiti to America on September 22, 1969, fleeing poverty and repression under the oppressive rule of dictator François Duvalier, also known as Papa Doc. My mother would soon come over once my father settled and earned enough money to bring her to America. He worked tirelessly to create a house and a home for my brother and me. I remember hearing him from time to time head to his union job at 4:00 in the morning. He worked a grueling morning and afternoon shift in the kitchen of a nursing home preparing meals for elderly patients.

Once home, he would quickly change clothes and start another one of his many jobs. This one was his own business. He started a cleaning company and hired other Haitian immigrants, who helped him clean various business offices and homes around town. On the days that I got to accompany him on his cleaning route, I remember us arriving home well after midnight. I could not help but think that while we both headed to bed exhausted from the long day, he was scheduled to wake up only a few hours later to repeat the grueling schedule once again. All in the name of his family.

Despite his toils, I grew up in an America that was still ambiguous about my father's entrance into this country. Thirteen years after my father's arrival in 1982, the Centers for Disease Control and Prevention (CDC) incorrectly described "being of Haitian origin" as a new risk factor for the sudden and tragic AIDS epidemic exploding in America. One year later, people were espousing "the 4H club," which described the likelihood of getting AIDS: homosexuality, hemophilia, heroin use (due to needle sharing), and *being of Haitian origin*.

The United States has always intertwined health policy with immigration policy. Even before the country was founded, the Articles of Confederation, ratified in 1781, describes in Article 4 that "free inhabitants" of each state "shall be entitled to all privileges and immunities"[1] denoting the difference between slaves brought to the United

States against their will and White settlers or indentured servants who migrated to America on their own volition. A pattern would soon emerge. The Immigration Act of 1891 allowed the United States to deny immigrants admission into our country based solely on the perceived presence of disease or illness.[2] This would become one of the earliest forms of racial profiling at the border.

Things would only get worse. In 1924, the United States implemented immigration quotas based on the immigrant populations already in the country as of the 1890 national census.[3] This rule would dramatically shrink immigrants as a percentage of the total U.S. population from 15% to 5% by the 1960s. Of course, these quotas would disproportionately impact immigrants of color.

After the assassination of Martin Luther King, Jr., the country began to change. Shortly after the passage of the Civil Rights Act of 1964, President Lyndon Johnson also signed into law the Immigration and Nationality Act of 1965. Finally, America's borders would be reopened and America's immigrant population would return back to nearly 13% of the U.S. population by 2010.[4] Although the perception evolved that most immigrants positively enhance our society, this same perception did not apply to Haitian immigrants. They would continue to face discrimination in America.

An evolutionary biologist named Michael Worobey discovered that HIV infections were occurring in the United States for 12 years before scientists first recognized AIDS as a disease in 1981.[5] HIV was first brought to Haiti from central Africa in 1966. It then made its way to America through major cities like Miami or New York and spread from there. Despite this history, a climate of increasing HIV/AIDS fear persuaded President Reagan to add HIV/AIDS to the registry of diseases that were barred entry into the United States. Twelve years later, President Clinton followed suit. As a result, an increasing stigma against Haitian immigrants spread throughout the country. In fact, in 1992, roughly 158 Haitians who had been granted asylum were instead detained in Guantanamo Bay indefinitely.[6]

To add insult to injury, the Food and Drug Administration (FDA) at the same time recommended that all blood banks refrain from accepting blood donations from any and all Haitians.[7] This new policy, grounded in discrimination and fear, galvanized thousands of Haitians to march and protest in the streets of New York City and Miami against such irrational policies. Such policies only increased the stigma, attacks, and discrimination against Haitian immigrants in America.

As a child, I had no idea what was going on, but I was to learn about xenophobia and understand the precautions looming over my parents and myself while living in New York. All I knew about Haiti back then was its volatile political past, its poverty, and its supposed origin of AIDS in America. My parents were tight-lipped about Haiti's history, although they loudly debated Haitian politics in their native tongue around the dining room table with extended family members. Since my family did not teach me about the history of the country they called home, I learned about it from other sources. I could feel America's disdain for my heritage and culture.

I remember being able to sense the animosity through gestures and stares. It would happen at the bank, while we waited for a teller to help my father deposit checks into his small business account. The bank tellers were nice and cordial, but I could tell they would count the people on the line to determine who would end up dealing with my father and me. Some would, from time to time, close down right as we arrived at the front of their line. There was one teller, an African American lady, who would look out for us. She would make eye contact with my father and with a nod convey: "Don't mind these crazy folks. I got you!"

Sometimes we would wait or let other people pass us in line to reach her teller station purposely. When we walked up, my father was always jovial. I could see he spoke confidently with his pronounced Haitian accent in these situations. Otherwise, he was demure and quiet and tried to avoid bringing attention to himself. But with this teller, whatever nervousness or intimidation he felt disappeared. Indeed, my dad had swagger.

When growing up and attending church, I could often detect a feeling of shame as well. We went to a very diverse church with people from a variety of countries and origins. When congregants found out that we were Haitian, they always sought to help us. In the church, we were encouraged to help, especially those less fortunate. However, *how* this help was given seemed to be always in public, always for show, and often in a way that fed the congregants' egos more than us in a practical way. I recall that when the church sought to collect food for the less fortunate in our community, my family always took part. I would eagerly go shopping with my mother to buy canned foods that we could deliver at the church's food drive each Sunday.

In Sunday school, our class would learn about the merits of giving back and the lesson was always tied to Luke 6:38: "Give, and it will be given to you. A good measure, pressed down, shaken together and running over, will be poured into your lap. For with the measure you use, it will be measured to you."

To me, this Bible verse was proof that it was important to give. However, who would have thought that our giving would have led to our receiving as well? One Christmas Eve while our family was away shopping, our fellow church members visited our home to give *us* food. At the time, our front door lock was broken, and my parents lacked the funds to fix it. With a little wiggling, anyone could enter the house. Since the lock was broken, when members of my church visited, they felt free to let themselves in, stuff our refrigerator, and cover our kitchen table with donated food.

Not in a million years did my family ever imagine we were donation targets from the same church to which we regularly donated! I remember coming home to find a note on the fridge declaring that our fellow church congregants let themselves in and gave us all this food for the holiday season. They prayed for us and wished us God's blessings. It was signed by some of the parents whose children were in my Sunday school class. I was mortified. In that moment, I came to realize the distinction between pleasantries and pity. The distinction between empathy and sympathy. The distinction between others' perception of you and your own.

We were the Haitian immigrants in that church who needed a helping hand. When I was a young boy, there was never a day my parents did not provide for me. While we were not the richest on the block, my parents did not use any social or governmental programs to make ends meet. Just blood, sweat, and tears. Yet our church saw us as the same poor immigrants who were being held in Guantanamo Bay.

When the world thinks of Haitians as being so lowly, you start to believe it yourself. Even if you don't want to.

I grew up ashamed of my culture and my father's native tongue. I didn't speak French or Haitian Creole in the house even though I knew many, many words when I was young. I was so embarrassed by my father's accent that I would run to answer the house's rotary phone in the kitchen to make sure no one else heard his accent over the phone. For some reason, I felt the need to spare random strangers and tele-marketers from hearing my dad's thick accent.

I wanted to fit in more with African Americans and distance myself from the Haitian and Caribbean communities. I had an insatia-ble need to assimilate. I had to fit in whatever the cost. When you stick out, you constantly have to explain yourself and your place in the world. It was exhausting. I just wanted to be myself.

It was not until I turned 12 that my seventh-grade English teacher, aware of my ethnic background, put a book in my hand and told me to read it. That book was *The Three Musketeers*.

When Alexandre Dumas wrote his famed masterpieces *The Count of Monte Cristo* and *The Three Musketeers*, many people do not know he was inspired by the stories of his father, Thomas-Alexandre Dumas Davy de la Pailleterie. Thomas-Alexandre Dumas was one of the highest-ranking men of African descent to ever lead a European army. He was also the first person of color to become a Divisional General and General-in-Chief in the French army. He was such a historic figure! In fact, Dumas was the highest-ranking officer of African descent in the Western world until 1975, when Daniel James Jr. achieved the rank of four-star general in the United States Air Force.

But the most important information that I learned was that Alexandre Dumas's father was born in Haiti just like my father. It brought me so much pride to learn the history of both Alexandre Dumas, the author, and his father, the general. How cool it was to know that the world's most famous swashbuckler, who has inspired so many Hollywood blockbusters, was born in Haiti and birthed by an enslaved Black woman named Marie-Cessette.[8] In one generation,

Thomas-Alexandre defied all odds, ascending from slavery to a top military post in Paris, France. Born in France, his son, Alexandre Dumas, would later make his father's legacy live on forever through the power of his pen in epic tales about his father's adventures. I could not even imagine what it must have felt like rising through the ranks of the French military as one of the only people of color, defiantly honoring his past by enlisting using his mother's surname, instead of his slave-owning father's name. Thomas-Alexandre was fearless in the face of it all.

It made me think about my father, who also left Haiti for a foreign land to give his son a better chance at life. Learning about the Dumas family helped me find my love for Haiti. Where once I was ashamed of my roots and my father's thick accent, I was now proud of my heritage and eager to learn more. Alexandre Dumas and I also had something in common: "All for one and one for all." This is the quintessential quote for anyone who is part of a team. I will always have my dad's back and find solace in the fact that he will always have mine. When that level of trust exists between a man and his boy, that boy has the audacity to think that anything is possible.

That is why it was hard for me to process our financial status as a child. Stuart Pierre was my hero, but when I tried to use our healthcare benefits at a dentist's office, I learned for the first time that he was also imperfect. Seeing my dad agonize over the fact that our dental benefits did not cover my root canal was an epiphany for me.

For the first time ever, I witnessed his uneasiness, insecurity, and, indeed, his humanness. At the time, he dared not let me know the reality, although it was written all over his face. I never knew how much of a defining moment this would be for my life. This experience would forever change me and my professional path. It became the impetus for my return to graduate school to study health policy and financial management. It became the bedrock of my healthcare career. I made it a point in my career to do my utmost to make sure that no one has healthcare benefit gaps when they visit their doctor. Never discount those defining moments in your life. Instead, use them as fuel to change the world.

LESSON 2.1: FIND YOUR ROOTS

The American history we learn in school does not tell the full story of people of color in this country—not by a long shot. Chinua Achebe, the famed Nigerian novelist and essayist, once said, "Until the lions have their own historians, the history of the hunt will always glorify the hunter."[9] This is true for many immigrants and people of color seeking their story in American history. Do not leave it up to chance to find out about your heritage or the great achievements of your ancestors. Seek out the history of your people so you can find pride and solace in those who look and speak like you, those who have come before you and achieved great things.

As debates rage on in school districts across the country about the type of history we should teach young American children, we can witness firsthand the hunter seeking to write history. It is the reason why 450 to 700 statutes and buildings glorifying Confederate soldiers were erected all across the South after the Civil War.[10]

Sachin H. Jain, MD, MBA

Recognized by Modern Healthcare *magazine as one of American healthcare's 100 most influential leaders*

"I was the first of my immediate family to be born in the United States. I experienced quite a bit of racism and feelings of otherness as a child growing up in northern New Jersey. My parents came here from India. We were the only individual unit of our extended family who had migrated to the United States. We stayed very close to our family in India. I would say my parents' heads and bodies were in the United States, but their hearts were back in India. There's a sense of sacrifice that comes through when your parents make the decision to move to a new world; a new country. Within that sacrifice, there is also a need to want to validate their choices. It was embedded in how we were raised that our job was to do better than our parents."

Our history is all around us—you just have to inform and educate yourself. Writer Ta-Nehisi Coates wrote the seminal work *Between the World and Me*, boldly reframing America's history in present-day context. James Baldwin was best known for exploring racial and social issues of his time in written works like *Notes of a Native Son* and *Nobody Knows My Name*. Additionally, Marie Arana has written about Simón Bolívar in *Bolívar: American Liberator*. Bolívar is most famously known for liberating six different Latin countries. And the esteemed Henry Louis Gates wrote *Black in Latin America*, which discusses the slave trade in colonial Mexico and how Cuba and Brazil became what they are today.

What you learn through these influential books and other ones like them is that the history of our world is very layered. My interest in Alexandre and Thomas-Alexandre Dumas led to even further research into the history of Haiti. Uncovering Haiti's great liberators like Jean-Jacques Dessalines, Henry Christophe, and Toussaint Louverture instilled in me a self-confidence that dramatically changed my worldview. I once thought my ancestors were destitute and uneducated. Quite the contrary, Haiti overcame Napoleon Bonaparte, the most powerful military general of the day, to gain its independence—the first Black republic in the world to do so.[11] Knowledge of such history changed me inside. I too became liberated from the negative thoughts and shame I once had about my family and the country my father called home. It's one of the reasons I became an executive producer of a documentary titled *1804: The Hidden History of Haiti* in 2017.[12] I wanted to share this knowledge with the world.

Once again, seek out the history of your family and your ancestry to discover heroes from your community. These examples should sustain and inspire you through your toughest times. If you can understand the triumphs of your past, you will be able to overcome any obstacles in your future.

LESSON 2.2: LEARN FROM YOUR HEROES AND SHEROES

There will be times you will face obstacles, setbacks, and difficulties, in your life and in your career. One of the benefits of being grounded in your roots and your heritage is learning from those who came before you. I've come to realize that even my worst days do not come close to the experiences my ancestors have endured. I am fully aware of my first-world problems. *If they did not give up, how can I?* The deeper your roots, the more powerful your life lessons will be. Watching my father wake up at 4:00 every morning and come home after midnight each night to keep a roof over our heads was one of my greatest lessons on the importance of having a strong work ethic. Learning about Haiti's fight for freedom, which took nearly 13 years, also instills the important of perseverance. Work ethic and perseverance are just two lessons I learned from my past that I take with me into my future.

You can also discover self-worth and pride. Discovering Jean-Michel Basquiat's Haitian background and Brooklyn, New York, roots was monumental for me.[13] As one of the world's most renowned painters, Basquiat and would go on to paint *Untitled* (1982), joining the likes of Pablo Picasso, Leonardo da Vinci, and Andy Warhol, who also have sold paintings for more than $100 million.[14] As you research your past, I'm sure you will find many more figures that will inspire you.

CHAPTER 3

Reclaim Your Seat

Reaching the Top Is Not as Difficult as Staying There

Success is not measured by the position one has reached in life, rather by the obstacles one overcomes while trying to succeed.
—*Booker T. Washington*

It was January 2018. I just accepted the position of chief operating officer at the largest health insurance company in New York. I was 35 years old. I had never made more money in my life. I was earning more than four times my parents' income combined. But they did not understand how to react. They were uncomfortable and even anxious. Both my mother and father were unsure whether they should be overjoyed or fearful for my future. Although they came to America to build a foundation for me, they could never have dreamed I would end up having a seat so close to the top. For them, this was akin to flying too close to the sun. They felt trepidation because my professional growth was quickly becoming disconnected from their own experiences and thus their tutelage. The fear within them was palpable. Because my parents had both faced real adversity like racism and financial hardships since coming to America, it was hard for them to fully understand how my achievements were possible in the same country that had essentially scorned them.

Often immigrant parents hold this baggage over their children in silence. Consequently, first-generation children carry this unspoken burden throughout their lives. *Be smart, but not too smart. Get A's but don't become the valedictorian of your class. Be the best, but don't act like you are. Don't seek attention. Be unseen and unheard. Be a good, quiet, obedient American citizen. Your actions weigh on us as much as they do on your future. Always make good decisions. Don't embarrass our family name.*

These were words I never explicitly heard from my parents, but the sentiments were strongly felt and understood. In the back of their minds, my parents questioned the ulterior motives of any company—particularly a profitable, publicly traded one that promoted someone so young, and, in their minds, so inexperienced, to such a high-level position. There must be some reason for my promotion other than my simply being qualified for this position. My parents never really understood what I did at work or my place in the company's hierarchy. In their heart of hearts, they prayed that I was not a token placed in this role merely to achieve diversity metrics. Even worse, they feared that I was a fall guy, a future scapegoat in a suit who would solely take the blame for the company's misfortunes. They had seen stories like this from Hollywood that made it seem all too possible.

"Why did they pick you?" my mother would ask me over and over again whenever I visited her during my first year as COO. "I don't know, Mom," was usually my standard reply.

Ironically, I honestly don't know why they hired me, but once I got the position, I too was scared to ask why. And with my new workload, I was too preoccupied to attempt to find out.

But I learned quickly that occupying a corner office is only the start of the journey to the top. Staying there is harder than I ever imagined. The real battle begins on your first day as you make sure you belong in the role. I suppose the biggest fear for Super Bowl winners is beginning the next season. There is only one way to go— and that's down, unless they repeat their victories and remain champions.

A 1995 psychology study by Medvec, Madey, and Gilovich found that Olympic bronze medal winners were always happier than silver medal winners when standing at the podium to receive their medals.[1] On a scale from 1 to 10 where 1 is agony and 10 is ecstasy, bronze medalists had an average score of 7.1 as compared to silver medalists, who scored 4.8. Reaching the top is absolutely an achievement, but just missing the top, even though you could be in the highly respected second place, brings about emotions of failure, shame, loss, and the erosion of one's self-confidence.

I have found that many women and people of color, including myself, at first do not believe they belong at the top. This is known as *Imposter Syndrome*. Even before they can worry about staying at the top, they spend undue energy trying to prove to themselves that their place there is not a fluke.

Imposter syndrome is described as the feeling of not being good enough for the role you are in, unsure of whether you are doing a competent job or satisfying the expectations of others. To put it simply, imposter syndrome is the experience of feeling like a phony: you feel as though at any moment you are going to be discovered as a fraud, that you don't belong where you are. It can affect anyone, whatever their social status, work background, or degree of expertise. However, it tends to disproportionately impact women and people of color— especially women of color. (Note that the two women who first coined the term, clinical psychologists Pauline Clance and Suzanne Imes, prefer the terminology "impostor phenomenon."[2])

I have certainly experienced imposter syndrome now and then. I had similar thinking with the same worry, fear, and intimidation I had as a newcomer to corporate America. Sometimes you can take the kid out of the cubicle, but the cubicle-level thinking can still pop up out of nowhere. However, over the years, I've been able to manage my imposter syndrome. To keep myself grounded, I remind myself that it is an unfair social construct to believe that professionals of color must be perfect to be hired or promoted. Or just to belong. While this social construct is pervasive in our society, it is wrong and must be combated at every stage of your career.

We herald all the firsts of Black America: from Barack Obama, the first African American President, to Kamala Harris, the first Asian American, African American, Caribbean American Vice President. All of these Black pioneers must confront something called the Jackie Robinson syndrome. It is a term I described (pseudonymously) in the book *Black Privilege: Modern Middle-Class Blacks with Credentials and Cash to Spend* by Dr. Cassi Pittman Claytor. I then stated: "If [Jackie Robinson] was spitting at people who were calling him the n-word, throwing stuff, getting mad at press conferences after the game, yeah, they would have been like, 'Shut it down. No more.' However, he had to be quiet. He had to take the hits. He had to be docile and behave in such a way that the baseball owners would exclaim about Black ballplayers: 'Yeah, look, they are not that bad. Let them in.'"[3]

Specifically, the term is used to describe the pedagogy that people of color have to be perfect to be considered for a leadership role. Jackie Robinson was not only the first African American to play in Major League Baseball, but he was also the Rookie of the Year in 1947. Barack Obama attended two Ivy League schools as a graduate of both

Columbia University and Harvard University. He was also the first Black person to be president of the *Harvard Law Review* in 1991.

If you are a person of color and you've been hired for a position, there's a high likelihood that you not only deserve to be there, you may be *overqualified*. Some of your peers most likely had an easier path, as seen in Figure 3.1. This myth of meritocracy is grounded in research. A 1987 Braddock and McPartland study of 4,078 employers found that entry-level minorities face four types of exclusionary barriers: "Segregated networks at the candidate stage of the application process, informational bias and statistical discrimination at the entry-level

Figure 3.1   The Myth of Meritocracy

Rashidi Hendrix

Owner, Producer, and Manager of Metallic Entertainment, a film, TV and music production company

"You know I can walk up to a total Black stranger. And I can talk to him and ask him about how White folks treat him on the job and he'll know exactly what I'm talking about. I may not even know this person, but that's part of the systemic racism history of the country. That's what we're dealing with. I think part of the problem is just that we don't interact with each other enough. We maybe have work friends and then after work we separate. . . . We don't really know each other."

stage, and closed internal markets at the promotional stage."[4] Thus, at every point of your career journey, you face higher barriers to professional growth than do your White counterparts.

From day one of my new job, I was forced to defy stereotypes and redefine what it means to be Black in corporate America. The statistics show that I am more likely to be underemployed, disproportionately laid off, and paid less than my White colleagues with the same education and experience. That's how I start my day. Each action I take can either validate or invalidate those generalizations, which means that I often start a meeting with ground to cover. When I walk in, my title and position in the company are not readily assumed. When I open my mouth, I am careful to be selective with my words to emote the 3Cs: *confidence*, *competency*, and *charisma*. This is the only way to ensure that I take full advantage of the power of first impressions.

Employees of color can spend so much time trying to exist in the roles they deserve that they do not spend enough time thinking about their future and excelling at their new job in the organization. The anxiety, emotions, and stress just to survive may also cause exhaustion and burnout.

I believe that many ethnically diverse employees also view their backgrounds as obstacles to their career aspirations. This is a major mistake. Do not focus on the qualities and capabilities you lack. Instead, be proud of the talents and skills you do possess. If employees of color can harness the lessons learned from growing up through adversity or in an immigrant household to thrive in the corporate environment, they will not only excel, but will become an even more valuable resource for their employers.

Unfortunately, many immigrants and employees of color do not regard their backgrounds and experiences as assets. They hide their distinctions from others. This is the trap in which many employees of color find themselves: in their attempts to assimilate, they shed everything that makes them distinctive and indeed, unique. This can lead to underperformance, discouragement, and dissatisfaction. *If employees of color don't value and nurture themselves, who in corporate America will?*

I recall vividly moments where my background became an asset in the boardroom. As COO, when meeting politicians, many of whom were people of color in New York, I felt their excitement as they discovered that I was an executive of color at such a high level. They were accustomed to seeing people of color at their events and their meetings, but not in the C-Suite, directly reporting to the CEO.

As one of the few employees of color on our executive steering committee working with a marketing agency hired to attract the Hispanic population, I was able to provide much needed guidance to their data analytics and insights. A Bronx resident for more than 16 years, I was also able to bring a dose of reality to internal meetings that tended to dehumanize our clients. Ivory tower thinking can keep you too many floors above the communities a company is trying to serve. Living in the Soundview section of The Bronx, I was always in the room (the right room) to ensure that our discussions focused on our impacted members. I wore that skill as a badge of honor.

The key is to not bother thinking about whether you belong in the seat you occupy, as this will consume your mind and erode your courage. Instead, find solace in the discomfort you feel as one of the few people of color in the room. It is not easy to just be yourself. Actually, I have found that as a person of color in corporate America, I was rewarded for being someone else. I received pay increases, promotions, and gained the trust of my senior leaders by being someone they were comfortable being around. For years, I contorted myself into a pretzel to appease my colleagues and win over their acceptance. I was safe, docile, agreeable, and amenable. All to a fault. But the more I did it, the higher up the ranks I rose. Similar to Pavlov's dogs, just a ring of a bell turned me into someone I was not in order to appease the crowd.

"You're not the smart. You're not that funny. And you're not that handsome." I heard these words spoken to me during my first weeks on the job as an executive from another Black executive concerned for my success and longevity at the company. His message was clear. Dim my light as to not shine too brightly among my peers. I excelled at doing this all so well . . . but eventually to a fault.

In America, it is indeed a privilege to be who you are in the workplace and have it work to your advantage. Conversely, there are diminishing returns to putting on a front for the higher-ups to accept you. Once you do get to the top, you will want to stay there, but to do this, your new peers around the executive table will want to see the person they have come to know. They have never met the real *you*. And that is the sacrifice you make, because when the company's leadership team can see you vulnerable, they will see you as more of a human. That will foster trust and increase your engagement with them. At the end of the day, you will become a more effective leader. Executives of color find themselves dancing between both realities.

For you to even have achieved corporate success as an employee of color, you most likely had to perform at levels above and beyond those of your peers. Now that you have arrived, it may seem like they now have even higher expectations. This juxtaposition is eye-opening, and it's important to prepare yourself for this before it happens. It's similar to transitioning from an individual contributor to a people leader. As an individual contributor, you were rewarded for being an expert, for being a specialist in your particular field, and for maintaining high individual performance levels. But as a people leader, your performance is based on a totally different standard. Now, the organization wants to see you curate an environment in which the individual contributors reporting to you can thrive. You are graded on your ability to get the most out of your people, your ability to transform ordinary teams into extraordinary forces. Successful managers can make this switch. Others will remain stagnant. They will not want to relinquish their manager title and compensation, but they still want the attention and work gratification of an individual contributor.

LESSON 3.1: BUILD YOUR PERSONAL BOARD OF DIRECTORS

To adequately prepare for success, you need to build a team. Call it your personal board of directors. These are the experts you surround yourself with who will help you get to where you are going. The best analogy I can use to describe the importance of such a team is a Formula 1 pit crew in auto racing. This is a tight-knit fleet of 20 highly trained professionals who stabilize and monitor your race car, changing tires and adjusting fluids as needed. Your success is tethered to their ability to keep you safe and your race car in tip-top shape. A successful pit crew in corporate American can include an executive coach, a personal therapist, mentors, champions, and colleagues in your social network who are more successful than you.

Your board of directors will help you prepare for success and hone your 3Cs. Many executives do not initially realize the pressure on the human mind, body, and spirit that exists as a person of color at the highest levels of corporate America and the toll it takes. The hours are grueling. You are always on, 24 hours a day, 7 days a week. When you are physically not working, your mind will be preoccupied with the needs of your business. You will wake up randomly in the wee hours of the morning, startled by a business concern that has been unresolved for far too long. As an executive, the decisions you make will never have a clear right or wrong answer. You will consistently be operating in the gray, weighing the pros and cons of a decision and thinking through unintended consequences.

When things go right, it will be due to your team. However, when things go wrong, it will be your fault, whether the failure was within your control or not. Having to answer for circumstances beyond your control is part of the price of executive leadership. As you make business decisions, you not only think about the financial, reputational, and operational aspects but also what that decision will mean for the employees in the company. Will there be layoffs? Will workload increases cause burnout and employee turnover? Are teams adequately trained and prepared for the change?

Decision-making at the executive level is a multivariate equation and there is never a right answer—just judgment calls based on limited data, previous experience, and a level of risk tolerance. As humans, we make more than 35,000 decisions every day.[5] Corporate executives invariably make even more. Each decision can carry weight and drain you as a leader.

LESSON 3.2: THERAPY IS PREVENTIVE MEDICINE

It is essential for executives of color to cope with their disproportionately high levels of stress and anxiety. Allow yourself a safe space to decompress and release the trauma of work without dumping on your loved ones.

Therapy is an excellent solution. Many think they do not need it until their stress levels impact the activities of their daily life. The first time I sought out therapy was when I started to physically feel my anxiety manifest as pain in my chest. By that time, I had been bottling up months and months of worries and fears about whether I belonged in my new work role. I should have started seeing a therapist earlier and more often. During the height of the pandemic, I was living alone, without any physical human contact for months. One of the ways I coped was through weekly therapy sessions. I am so thankful that I began therapy before the pandemic started because I had a therapist to call in my time of need.

Resources

- BEAM—Black Virtual Wellness Directory: https://wellness .beam.community/
- Therapy for Black Girls— https://therapyfor-blackgirls.com/
- Therapy for Latinx—https:// www.therapyforlatinx.com/
- Inclusive Therapists (BIPOC)— https://www.inclusivether-apists.com/
- ZenCare—https://zencare.co/ us/new-york/therapists/ identity/asian

Unfortunately, therapy is still a stigma in many communities of color. If chronic stress goes unchecked and overloads you to the point that you are unable to cope, poor health outcomes such as hypertension and obesity can result. Researchers call this *allostatic load*, and once again, it disproportionately impacts people of color.[6] It is unfortunate that more people of color don't appreciate the benefits of therapy. I was skeptical at first but have since healed myself after meetings with a behavioral health professional. My chest pains subsided, and I learned breathing exercises to handle any incoming anxiety attacks. I also have improved my quality of sleep at night. I owe it all to my therapist.

LESSON 3.3: GET A COACH!

I also recommend getting a superb executive coach. Some may think your therapist can be your coach, but I argue that they should be two different people with distinct perspectives. Although the cost for an executive coach may be a concern, there is a chance your employer may pay for it, especially if the focus of the engagement is aligned to your growth in the company. Their impact is immeasurable, so even without support from your job, it is still a worthy investment into yourself and your career. My executive coach helped me to strategically think through work situations and decide how to handle them. He made sure I understood the feedback I was receiving from my peers. My coach also delineated the gap between the executive I wanted to become from where I currently stood. Our conversations never veered into personal or family discussions. I reserved those conversations for my therapist. The greatest lesson I had to learn was that I am not as good as my best day, but I am also not as bad as my worst day. As an employee of color, I put so much pressure on myself to perform, knowing that failure is not an option. With my coach's help, I am able to detach myself from my work performance. I can attest to the powerful benefits of having an executive coach in your corner.

CHAPTER 4

Harness Your Distinctions

The First Time You Discover Your Racial Identity Is Life-Transforming

To be a Negro in this country and to be relatively conscious is to be in a rage almost all the time.

—James Baldwin

Most people of color in America have imprinted on their psyche a memory of the first time they felt out of place. This defining moment usually occurs when you first encounter racial discrimination, profiling, or bias. I remember mine vividly.

I was five years old and in my Sunday school class. I raised my hand and asked to go to the bathroom. As I walked in, I saw an older Sunday school student in the restroom. We both used the urinals and then made our way to the sinks to wash our hands. As I gathered soap and lathered my hands together, the student looked over at me and stared. I looked back at him awkwardly, wondering what he was looking at. That's when he asked, "Why're your palms lighter than the rest of you?"

This had never occurred to me. I'd never consciously recognized the color difference on my hands. I shrugged, not knowing the answer. He then went on to say that every time I wash my hands, the soap and water must be washing off some of my skin color.

Aha! That's why the color on my palms appears to fade away.

Denise J. Brown

Entertainment Attorney and Former Senior Vice President of Warner Bros. Records

"I went to Brooklyn Law School. That first week there, racism slapped me in my face from every direction, whether it was other students or from people that worked there. But that first week was a very, very difficult week. I remember coming home and crying every night. Calling my mom and saying, "I can't do this. They're looking at me as if I don't belong here." But she wasn't hearing it. She replied, "Show these people what you're made of. Show them that you do deserve to be there and you're not just filling a quota." That was a very pivotal week because it could've gone either way."

One of the hardest things about being part of a marginalized group is getting used to the questioning and prodding about your existence in the world. Like you're a real-life science project that members of the *normal* group are free to comment on out loud, claiming entitlement in asking what others would consider inappropriate to ask.

This places you at an important fork in the road. Do you accept your fate and answer questions at will? Do you decline to participate in this game of questioning? I judiciously decide on a case-by-case basis whose questions to entertain based on the authenticity of the inquirer. Truth be told, it's exhausting.

That day when I was five, the fear of my color fading away made me decide I'd never take a bath again. I'd go on a bathing boycott without telling my parents—at least for the few weeks until they literally forced me into the bathtub. But I was too embarrassed to tell my parents why; I decided to tuck my fear of losing my skin color into my heart, and I've never told anyone until now.

The next prominent racial memory I have was the first time I was called the *n-word*. I was an eighth-grader playing for my school's basketball team. I'd heard the word a million times before from friends, rap songs, and just living in a predominately Black community. But hearing it come from a strange White basketball player as he fouled me to the ground shattered my sensibilities. He said it with so much intention, so much anger. I had never heard it in that tone and diction before. I played for an all-Black school, and our league competed against schools in our district of mostly White students. Whenever our bus arrived for away games, we were always met with stares as we disembarked. It was in stark contrast to seeing NBA players arrive at arenas across the country, greeted by long lines of cheering fans trying to just catch a glimpse of their basketball idols. Nobody cheered when we got off the bus.

NBA players wear their Beats by Dre headphones and dark sunglasses to avoid the rush of the crowds awaiting their arrival. I wish I had had those shields at the ready to help me ignore the dirty stares and whispers that enveloped us when we arrived. No headphones, no sunglasses, no back entrance for us. No—upon arrival, we were subjected to this slow march into the host gyms and forced to hear every single insult that was spit at us. Forced to accept every stare that came our way. What was the real difference between us eighth-graders and those NBA stars?

Let's see. High school basketball player—not good. Dangerous. Thuggish. Aggressive. If not for this, they would be on the street. NBA basketball player—very exciting. Talented. Famous. You should be just like them when you grow up.

I not only heard the word said out loud by the White player, *I felt it*. Even though I was fouled hard and eventually fell to the ground with a thud, it was that n-word that actually hurt the most. It pierced through me like a dagger. As I got up from the gym floor, the referee blew the whistle—only a regular run-of-the-mill foul! My blood began to boil, and I became overcome with rage. Rage at the foul, rage at what just happened, and rage at the referees for not calling a flagrant or technical foul. I lunged at the boy, pushed him hard, and knocked him to the floor. That was precisely when the deafening noise of a whistle silenced the court again and left me standing as stiff as a deer in headlights.

The call: technical foul on *me*. I uttered a few curse words in disbelief. My coach shot up from the bench and ran over to calm me down. My Black teammates seemed more concerned with my demeanor at that interminable moment than the egregious call we'd just witnessed. They too begged me to calm down and brush it off. But it was too late. One more technical foul was called, and I was ejected from the game. Adding to my burning rage was the fact that my middle finger was throbbing like crazy. When I'd stretched my hand to break my fall, I'd broken my finger.

Although this took place on a middle school basketball court, it served as a microcosm of the plight of people of color in and out of the workplace. The punishment for violations against you are subtle, yet the penalties for your reactions are always more severe. People of color are constantly asked to turn the other cheek and be the bigger person, whatever their age. What I learned on that basketball court will always haunt me. For the rest of my life, society will not just expect me to walk on eggshells, to act mature, to forgive and be emotionally intelligent—but will also demand me to *comply*. My life depends on it. This lesson helped me navigate the most defining racial memory of my life, which was soon to happen.

As a senior in college, I was "stopped and frisked" at gunpoint by police on the streets of The Bronx more times than I could count. The first time I trembled in fear. By the time I graduated, it had become a routine dance. The uniformed officers would inevitably ask for identification, and I would reluctantly produce my driver's license and Fordham ID card—always both.

Stop-and-frisk was a New York Police Department (NYPD) racially biased profiling policy that led to the temporary detention, questioning, and often search of New Yorkers just living their daily lives—whether they were suspects of a crime or not. My most severe altercation with the NYPD left me lying on a cold street in The Bronx one night at 11 p.m. My cheek was pressed between the concrete sidewalk and the knee of a New York City police officer paid to serve and protect me from the very same people he suspected me of being. He was twice my size, and he used all of his body weight to pin me to the ground despite my lack of resistance. I remember the incident so clearly that the neighborhood sounds still whisper in my ears. The onlookers with their pointing fingers already condemning me. The corner bodega boys who scattered once the police sirens turned on. The cars that slowed down as they passed through the intersection of 183rd Street and Arthur Avenue, trying to get a glimpse at was happening under the glaring luminescence of streetlamps.

This corner was known to Fordham students as the "Bermuda Triangle" because there were three bars and a pizza shop at each point of the intersection. It was far enough away from campus to be cool, but close enough for drunken Fordham students to make their way home without being assaulted. Many Fordham students circled around the triangle as they traveled from one bar to another before ending at the pizza joint at 2 a.m.

As I lay on the ground considering my fate, it was in that unending moment that I realized I was truly Black in America. Guilty before proven innocent. At first, I was embarrassed; in fact, mortified. For the next few years, I told no one.

I was arrested because I matched a broad description of a Black male suspect with blue jeans and a white T-shirt. No height specifications or any other description, not even facial features to speak of. Just a generic young Black man sought in connection to a recent stabbing that had occurred nearby. This wrongful arrest led police to issue me a Class E felony charge of resisting arrest.

Resisting arrest! I was arrested by plainclothes policemen who offered no reason whatsoever as to why I was being stopped, or whom he and his fellow police officers were pursuing. Resisting becomes the first logical action when strangers step out of a car and put their hands on you. I remember realizing that I would live longer if I complied even though the police officers had yet to identify themselves. But that is exactly when I voluntarily went to the ground and put my hands in front of my head, signaling the white flag.

Despite this gesture of peace, two officers still tackled me hard even though I was already on the pavement. I know they barked orders, but I don't recall what they said. They were loud, burly, and abrupt. Menacing in an almost demonic way. I just remember letting my body loosen so they could whip me around like a rag doll until tight cuffs were placed around my wrists.

I'd never thought about how it might feel to be shoved into the back of a cop car in front of a crowd wondering who I was and what had happened. When a police officer places his hand on your head as he guides you into the back seat, you immediately realize you're powerless. To begin with, the back seat of a police car is covered with hard plastic, so it's extremely uncomfortable. The way your arms are sadistically handcuffed behind you makes your shoulders hurt. The metal handcuffs are angled just right to dig into your wrists, causing maximum discomfort and pain. And it's hard to keep yourself upright since you can't use your arms and hands to hold yourself steady.

I remember trying to reason with the police and let them know I was a Fordham University student-athlete. That my ID card was in my wallet. It was my only evidence beyond the gates of Fordham University to exclaim to society that *I was a different type of Black person*. Without one, I was just a Black kid on Fordham Road. With it, I was an educated student-athlete at a prestigious Division 1 college trying to obtain an education and avoid becoming yet another statistic. *Same damn kid.*

What is the price to pay for fitting such a description? I paid attorney fees in excess of $5,000, which my family and I couldn't afford. I had to assemble character witnesses from all around Fordham University. Those who would be willing to testify in-person and through written affidavits attesting to my character. Eventually, I even persuaded a student eyewitness to testify on my behalf. She nervously accepted, knowing full well what could happen if I was found guilty of a felony charge. I would have to drop out of college, no longer run track, and walk through life with a criminal record that would serve as an albatross around my neck for the rest of my days on this planet. In a blink of an eye, everything in my life could change.

I could not imagine what transpired for other Black and Brown boys just like me who could not afford an attorney and lacked people of stature to vouch for their character. In most cases, they plead down their case and accept their unjust sentences. According to a study from the New York State Association of Criminal Defense Lawyers and the National Association of Criminal Defense Lawyers, 99% of all misdemeanors and 94% of all felony charges are resolved by a guilty plea.[1] These are the souls who end up populating prisons in America. To add insult to injury, approximately 90% of all stops based on a suspicion of a crime in New York involve people of color.

Fortunately, I was a member of the 6% minority of felony cases. My case was dismissed. But before I could celebrate, the judge told me my arrest record wouldn't be expunged until after 10 years of "good service." That is, 10 years with no further crimes or infractions.

I was a 21-year-old senior in college—a soon-to-be college graduate with a waiting job offer at the largest health insurance company in New York. Yet, for the next 3,650 days, I would effectively be paralyzed as I navigated the streets of New York. My then goal: to avoid a New York City police force that was hell-bent on targeting young Black males. In fact, in 2005, the year of my graduation, there were 398,191 stop-and-frisk incidents in New York

City.[2] Of those, 352,348 (89%) of these individuals were found completely innocent; 196,570 (54%) of them were Black, even though we only represented 25% of the population in New York City that year.[3] One of those incidents involved me. In fact, my Fordham hood was considered one of the top five neighborhoods in New York City where stops were done with a use of force 44.9% of the time.[4] Whenever you read or hear about a statistic, remember that behind those alienating numbers are red-blooded human beings with real lives, hopes, and dreams.

This one event changed my entire life. The freedom of spirit I had before my arrest was divine. But then it was gone. Everything changed that day. How I talked, what I wore, where I went, and what I did all changed. Despite being an aspiring hiphop artist at the time with a record deal from Right Move Records and opening up for artists like Three 6 Mafia, I had to change. It was imperative not only to avoid any criminal activity, but I also had to avoid the mere perception of impropriety while I lived my daily life. This was all in a focused effort to stay away from ever matching a criminal's description for the next 10 years. This defining moment in my life changed the lens through which I viewed the world forever. Believe me, I would never be the same.

I now teach young men and women that they too will have a defining story in their lives when they discover their racial identity in America. Mine was a sobering moment, and I wish I'd been better prepared for it. I also know I bring this trauma with me into the workplace. The lens through which I view the world has forever been skewed by my experience. I too have to ensure that my biases don't creep in when I react to certain situations, seeing problems where they may not exist.

Whatever your race, creed, or color, I am sure you have a story of an identity-defining moment in your life. It could be more or less traumatic than mine. But the goal for sharing is not to create a sufferer's Olympics. It is to find solace in others who also feel like outsiders in a society they too call their own. It's also to harness the knowledge gained through such an experience in order to better navigate life, because such moments are bound to happen again. In corporate America, the altercations are less physical—yet they can be just as mentally and psychologically draining.

Systemic racism in America is real, but please do not waste precious moments of your life trying to control it or prove its existence to those around you. You can only control how you react to racism, not the fact that it occurs. Since racism and bias exist in our society, it makes sense that they'll also appear in the workplace—a reality that for some reason is insanely difficult for corporations to acknowledge and address. Rather than spending sweat equity trying to prove or disprove bias in the workplace, executives should agree on its existence and spend their energy rooting it out.

In the workplace, racism can come in many forms, including microaggressions. Dr. Chester Middlebrook Pierce, a tenured Harvard Medical School professor of education and psychiatry, first coined the term in the 1970s.[5] Chet, as they called him, grew up in Glen Cove, New York, a predominantly White neighborhood, and became the *first* of many different attributes in his lifetime. The first Black senior class president at Glen Cove High School. The first Black American to play football at University of Virginia, an all-White university, as a member of the Harvard College football team. And the first Black professor at Massachusetts General Hospital.[6] Back then, Chet described microaggressions as "Black-White racial interactions [that] are characterized by

Toyin Ajayi

Co-Founder and CEO of Cityblock Health, a healthcare start-up valued at $5.7 billion focused on improving the health in underserved urban communities

"I mean there's nothing like the systemic and in-depth, baked-in legacy of the enslavement of people and the subsequent treatment of race in this country. I just never experienced anything like that anywhere on the planet. The layers upon layers of race and racism and the way that it's been woven implicitly into everything is really unique to this country. That doesn't mean that racism doesn't exist in other places, and certainly I've experienced racism in lots of different geographies across the world. But there is something very singular about racism in the United States that I think is quite insidious, pervasive and continues to be perpetuated."

Lucy M. Lopez

General Counsel and Chief Legal Officer at Spencer Stuart, a leading global executive search and leadership advisory firm.

"The microaggressions have been plentiful and frequent, both professionally and personally. They have been a part of daily life and I just accepted them and kept going, because if you stop to think about them, you'd be either pretty angry or confronting people all the time. It would exhaust me. An example from my personal life was when I bought my home in the suburbs of New York. I was a young lawyer at the time, maybe 29 years old. My new neighbors came over while I was outside with my young son. The question I got rather quickly past "hello" was: "Are you the nanny?" It requires so much of us to look beyond these things to help politely dispel the notion that I can't possibly be a young Hispanic professional who owns a house."

white put-downs, done in an automatic, preconscious, or unconscious fashion."[7]

One can only assume the term Chet coined was based on his amazing ascent professionally while navigating places where he was the only person of color. The term has since been expanded to include more ethnic groups and to highlight the power imbalance that exists between various groups in America. Today, 80% of BIPOC employees have experienced microaggressions in the workplace—and that's probably too conservative an assessment.[8] In later chapters, I discuss specific and pragmatic tactics for confronting racism and bias in the work environment.

LESSON 4.1: HARNESS YOUR IDMs

IDMs are the *Identity-Defining Moments* in your life that redefine your definition of race in America and what it means to be a person of color. These are critical moments of self-discovery, the turning points that change how you identify yourself forever. For me, that moment was when I got arrested. Up until that moment, I was young and invincible. After that moment, my world had changed. I'd realized the power of stereotypes, bias, and discrimination. My first reaction to all this was hesitancy and shame. It took me several years to work through that shame and to instead harness that identity-defining moment. The best way to harness such a traumatic moment in your life is through a process called the *Triple A*:

- *Acknowledge*

- *Accept*

- *Ascend*

First, you must *acknowledge* the trauma head-on. Say the story out loud. Tell a friend. Write it down. Acknowledgment will help you manage the anxiety, flashbacks, and mood swings you'll feel as memories return without solicitation. It took me a few years, but eventually I was able to write about my arrest using poetry, rhymes, and spoken word. Writing it down definitely helped me process the anger, shame, denial, and self-blame I felt. Holding in these feelings can lead to depression, isolation, or anger. If you are holding on to pain from a tragic situation, realize that the trauma will follow you everywhere. Acknowledgment is the first step toward healing and reconciliation.

Second, aim to *accept* the world as it is, flaws and all. Once I acknowledged my arrest, I went on a rampage in my early 20s trying to save the world from police brutality. While you can make change in the world through protests, volunteering, mentoring, and other acts of kindness, it's important to remember that it is not your job to save the planet. It sounds harsh, but it's an exercise in futility to attempt to be the social justice warrior in your workplace. Don't argue with the ignorant. Choose your battles wisely. Invest in people where you will get the greatest return. Far too often, I've seen employees become distracted by every rebuff they come across in the office and end up fighting wars on too many fronts. The key is to accept that the world is not perfect. I don't mean to forgive the world for being racist. I don't mean to forget the hardship that you suffer because of it. And I don't mean to allow the world to remain exactly as it is. I do think we can change the world in our own little ways, but real sweeping change is beyond one person. It is very hard to change hearts and minds. The key is to focus on creating an atmosphere that attracts and rewards allies who can become proponents of a more inclusive and equitable workplace with you. Strength in numbers is an age-old strategy. And it works. Do not fight alone. Become part of a coalition.

Third, take what you've learned from your IDMs, and *ascend.* Rise above those identity-defining moments and make a new reality for yourself. *The kid in The Bronx who was arrested in senior year of college became a COO.* Redefine what it means to recover from a setback. Ascension truly means using your past as fuel to propel you to your future. My IDM makes me unique rather than unqualified. My resiliency to overcome such adversity should help me leapfrog my peers rather than be a liability. Rather than being devalued by adversity, my commitment to my community should distinguish me. This is how to turn trauma into triumph. I know too many employees of color who are unable to ascend and who stay stuck in a revolving door of sadness and despair. Rise above the pain and don't let this happen to you.

LESSON 4.2: GUARD AGAINST EXCESSIVE SKEPTICISM

I had the unique opportunity to virtually meet Pamela Newkirk, author of *Diversity, Inc.: The Failed Promise of a Billion-Dollar Business.* She described to a group of executives how diversity at the top has largely remained unchanged for close to five decades. It can sometimes feel like even if you change jobs, the prospects of a better environment will still seem slim. *Same shit, different logo.*

In fact, a study from Fortune magazine found that only 3% of Fortune 500 companies release complete data for the race and gender of their employees in each job category and management. That means that 97 out of every 100 companies keep us in the dark on whether their organizations match the customers they serve and the employees they hire![9]

Despite those statistics, a 2018 McKinsey study found that *diverse companies perform 33% better financially.*[10] How do we reconcile these two facts? Corporations were built to make money in our capitalistic society. Research proves that diverse companies perform better financially. And yet, we still find ourselves with diversity metrics that have largely remained the same for the past few decades. When a company lacks diversity, there is less comfort and trust between races and cultures. When lower-level employees do not see any hope of moving up, they explicitly become jaded or disgruntled.

While there are valid merits to throwing in the towel and giving up, I personally encourage another tactic. In the face of adversity, wherever you are in your organization, do what you can to advance the ball in your own little way. If you're a line manager, make sure you counsel and motivate your employees of color to reach for higher heights. Profess to your teams that you have an open-door policy and create an environment in which employees feel comfortable coming to you. Hire diverse employees if you are in a position to do so; if you're not, make it a point to provide positive feedback about employees of color to their bosses on an ongoing basis. Be intentional. Give tangible examples. Even from a position of underrepresentation, there are things we can do to advance diversity and change the company culture.

Bruce Jackson

Associate General Counsel and Managing Director, Strategic Partnership, Microsoft
Author of Never Far from Home

"We need to hire diverse candidates—they're out there. When we talk about our hiring people who are non-diverse, we hire them based on potential. When it comes to diverse candidates, you have to have a position for maybe six months before they give it to you. We have got to start promoting diverse candidates the same way we promote all other candidates—based on potential."

CHAPTER 5

Job Interviews Happen Every Day

How Shampoo Changed My Life and Started My Career

> I am not ashamed of my past. I am not ashamed of my humble beginning.
>
> —*Madam C. J. Walker, first Black female millionaire*

My very first job was unpaid, but it ended up being the best job I could ever imagine. It is why I am where I am today. All jokes aside, shampoo changed my life.

When I was seven years old, I begged my father to see the epic movie thriller, *Teenage Mutant Ninja Turtles*, which was a gigantic hit in 1990. Thankfully, he obliged. One of the main characters of the film, Leonardo the blue Ninja Turtle, captivated me.

The Ninja Turtles consisted of four brothers: Leonardo was the leader of the group, Michelangelo was the class clown, Donatello was the nerdy tech whiz, and Raphael was the challenger of the group. Leonardo was always the most mature Turtle and his brothers looked up to him. Their karate master, Splinter, expected more from Leonardo than the others and that inspired me—even as a child.

Blissfully leaving the theater after the movie, we happened to pass a Tiger Schulman's Karate School. I remember begging my father to stop inside to collect information about joining. I wanted to be Leonardo, and I was hooked! I wanted to learn karate and be a leader. My dad hesitated at first, but eventually, he gave in to my pleading.

I started as a seven-year-old white belt, and it took me five years of consistent training and sparring competitions to finally graduate with a first-degree black belt. Along the way, I learned self-discipline and self-confidence and understood the benefits of hard work and service. Getting a black belt is a high honor in Tiger Schulman's Karate School. You become what is called a Sempai, a senior member of a group in Japanese martial arts—a mentor. Despite the high honor, Sempais quickly learn servant leadership. Sempais were expected to give more than they got. We were also expected to volunteer our time to clean the dojo and help teach classes, while continuing to train, learn, and sharpen our own techniques. I soon began to mentor and coach karate students in and out of the classroom. That is how I met a young student named Tony. Tony was shorter than the other kids his age, which left him a bit intimidated and shy. He also was very rambunctious and distracted. Somehow, Tony and I bonded. When he came to my Saturday morning class, he always made it a point to give me a high-five. Even when he would occasionally act up, I only had to look at him, and he would stop and behave.

After some time, Tony introduced me to his father. His father was very cordial, saying, "Thank you for how much you have helped our Tony." I was flabbergasted at his comment. *How had I helped Tony?* But his father later explained that his son's behavior had been improving since he started classes with me, and he was becoming better at following directions in and out of the classroom. Tony's father commended me on my teaching skills and was curious about what I charged for my services. I explained to him that this was my expected contribution as a Sempai. Surprised at my passion and dedication for a job that did not pay, he offered me an opportunity to earn some money. Tony's father was a partner in a beauty salon and supplies store at a nearby mall. He said that if I had an interest, he would be more than happy to hire me when I wasn't teaching at the karate school.

I was curious about what skills I could bring to a beauty salon and supply store, particularly as a young, untrained male adolescent. But I said yes. I started out in the warehouse, where I worked with an older, heavyset guy named Frank. He drove an old, brown, dilapidated delivery truck. We would pick up shampoos, conditioners, and other beauty supplies from the warehouse and distribute them to the various store locations. I would also wait for the delivery of supplies to the warehouse and help unload, sort, and stock them.

The job was fun, but there was a lot of waiting involved as shipments were often delayed. I decided to use this time to read the back information on those hair care bottles I was stocking. Slowly, I began to learn about all the brand-name shampoos our stores carried: Matrix Biolage, Redken, Nexxus, and Sebastian shampoos—what their ingredients were and what types of hair each product tried to cater to. There were so many!

I also took the time to reorganize the warehouse by product type and name and streamline our stocking process so we could pack the truck more efficiently. The urge to learn and innovate came from boredom. Rather than just sitting around waiting for a late shipment, I decided to improvise and fix the things that demanded attention.

When Stacy, one of the salon managers, found out that I was studying the products, she implored my boss to move me out of the warehouse and up to the front desk. My job would be rather simple. I would ring up customers at the register, vacuum at the end of the day, take out the trash, break down empty boxes, and stock shelves when necessary.

At first, I was nervous. *What was a young Black kid doing in the front of an upscale hair salon?* But over a few months, my comfort level grew and grew. Months changed into years, and by the time I was in high school, I was teaching less karate and earning more money at the store. I even began to close the store on weekend nights. This helped me gain the confidence to man the store by myself after high school track practice ended. I would close both registers at the end of the night and reconcile the proceeds with that day's receipted items. This was the highest form of trust my boss could offer me: managing his money.

After gaining acceptance to Fordham University in The Bronx, I decided to continue working at the store on Sundays. During these shifts, I worked with an eccentric diva of a hairdresser named Bobby, who had a love-hate relationship with his customers. On this particular Sunday, a customer was less than thrilled with her hair coloring and wash and blow. She expressed her dissatisfaction to him and refused to pay. The disagreement escalated and voices got louder as tempers flared. Every second of the argument felt like an hour, and I felt compelled to step in. I ran over to calm the customer down while the line at the register in the front of the store began to lengthen. I told her she did not have to pay for the cut and color, but I would not give her a refund. Instead, she would receive store credit and would need to return to repair her haircut with a different hair stylist. I was working on the fly here, having never encountered a situation like this before.

I then walked over to Bobby, the hairdresser, and assured him that he would get full payment for his services. He was already angry, and I knew he would explode if he thought he would not be compensated. I then ran back to the front of the store to serve the other customers waiting on line to pay. The disgruntled customer ended up choosing another hair stylist to finish the job. She picked a new time and date, and I logged it in the calendar. *Crisis solved*. Problem averted. Bobby later called our boss to complain about what I did. However, my boss was pleased with my split-second decision-making.

Later in the day, one of our regular customers, Suzy, came up to the front of the store to pay. Suzy was a quiet, unassuming woman. As she paid her bill, she complimented me on how well I had handled the situation. She was impressed with my ability to mediate two emotional middle-aged folks at my young age. I thanked Suzy for the kind words and from that point on, I always made it a point to greet her when she came to the store.

On a subsequent visit, Suzy asked me if *this* was all I did. She deduced that I must be up to more than managing a beauty salon and supply store on Sundays. I told her I was currently a sophomore at Fordham University pursuing a degree in finance. I could tell Suzy was thrilled at this news, and she then asked me if I'd be interested in an internship. Of course I would! After replying yes, she asked me to send her a copy of my resume. I didn't have one, but I told her I would send it to her as soon as I got home from work. She gave me her business card. I took it and stared. Suzy worked for the largest health insurance company in New York State. Underneath her name was her title: Chief Operating Officer (COO).

I did not know what that meant when I first glanced at it. I heard of a Chief Executive Officer or CEO, but never a COO. In those days, our phones lacked Internet access, Google was nonexistent, and our computers still suffered from "dial-up" speeds. So I never investigated what her title meant or what she actually did at the company. I soon reached out and sent her a copy of my newly created resume. After a few weeks, an email finally arrived in my inbox. It was an invite to visit the office for an interview.

Suzy's corporate office was on 42nd Street in a huge skyscraper, which to me was larger than life. No one in my family had ever worked for a big corporation. They definitely did not work in an office building in Manhattan. I bought two suits on sale for $99 on Fordham Road in The Bronx and tried to look my best for this interview. As I arrived, I was introduced to Suzy's executive assistant and asked to wait. I had finally looked up the company in the library the day before and now began to recall all the information I had gleaned. I knew their mission statement, company vision, and the well-known statistics about their reputable brand. I carefully studied the different health plans they sold and how long they had been in business. I also was aware of how many employees they had at the time—5,500 employees seemed like such a large number to me. Before this, I had only worked with three employees at Tiger Schulmann's and no more than eight employees at the beauty salon. This new gig was exponentially larger than I could have ever imagined.

I walked into the COO's office and scanned the giant space filled with plaques, a conference room table, and an immense window looking over the New York City skyline. I immediately realized she was a big deal. *The real deal.* It was kind of bizarre to see her in this light, as I usually saw her with curlers in her hair under a hot air dryer. Now in a corporate pantsuit behind a big desk, Suzy continued to be welcoming and cordial. She told me I would meet with various folks on her team.

When I met different individuals from various departments, I told them I was interested in finance. They soon partnered me with the budgeting team. I would start the following week! I quickly realized that this was less of an interview and more of a meet-and-greet. It suddenly hit me how much of an opportunity this had become—an opportunity that came about because of my actions on some random day at a hair salon where I surely didn't belong at first. *Shampoo changed my life.*

I began interning for Suzy's company and would stay there throughout the rest of my college tenure. My track and field coach approved the internship. At first, I was interning one day a week, during our rest days from track practice. However, toward the end of my junior year, I started interning three days a week. By my senior year, I was working five days a week and had full projects assigned to me.

I ended up receiving an offer letter from the company in the fall of my senior year. I was the first of all my roommates to have a bona fide job offer in hand. I remember discussing the job offer with my parents. In 2005, I would earn $31,000 a year to be a Product Analyst reporting to a Senior Analyst on the product development team. My parents were shocked by the offer. My father was perplexed at how I could be offered so much money without any proven skills or knowledge in health insurance. They wanted me to accept immediately and were shocked that I had not already done so.

If it hadn't been for mentors in my life whom I trusted, I would have never known about the concept of a counteroffer. Since I had also applied for full-time positions at other companies that spring, I was fortunate enough to be sitting on multiple offers. For example, a clothing company offered me a starting salary of $34,000, and a bank offered me $39,500.

Despite great apprehension, I told the hiring manager, Greg, that "Even though I am absolutely humbled by this job opportunity and the prospects of joining the team, I have another offer on the table that is a bit more lucrative." Greg gazed at me for a moment and then quickly took it in stride. He smiled and told me that he really wanted me on the team. Even though the days between the first offer letter and the updated one felt like months, I would soon receive a revised offer letter with a starting salary of $41,500!

I was ecstatic. This would be my first *real* professional job with benefits, and I would be making more money than my father. It was inconceivable. My father was so happy for me. It was really the main reason he came to America in the first place. I'll never forget that joyful call when I delivered the good news to him. He said, "Praise God!" and then demanded that I accept this offer at once before they came to their senses. This is how I started my journey in healthcare. One day a karate kid in a beauty salon met a COO.

LESSON 5.1 EVERY DAY IS AN INTERVIEW FOR YOUR NEXT PROMOTION

Whether you realize it or not, you are always being watched. It is important to act as such. You never know when you will meet someone who can change your life. The reality is that managers and people leaders are always looking for good talent, whether or not they are actively recruiting for a specific open position. You should approach every day at work as if it is your first day on the job. Come to work with the same energy, vigor, and passion that you had on that very first day. If you perceive your job as continually interviewing for your next position, you will approach issues and projects on a mission to excel.

One of the ways to stand out is to strive for excellence and continuously reinvent your role. In any job you have, regardless how menial it is, make it new and fresh. Do it differently than the ones that came before you. Stretch the role bigger than it was when you found it. Those are the tangible ways to separate yourself from the pack and create some distinction in the eyes of your managers.

Far too often, employees believe they deserve promotions based on tenure. They have done the same job for multiple years and now want a new title or pay raise because of their expertise. The true question is, how did you redefine the role? How did you make the processes more efficient? How did you add value to the role? Is the role still done in the exact same way as it was on your first day? These are key questions to answer before asking for a promotion.

You'll also have to be logistically ready for that new position. Is your resume updated? If you do get a new opportunity, have you thought about your salary requirements? Are you prepared to counter the initial offer? A good range for a counteroffer is anywhere from 10% to 20%. Many people of color and women are uncomfortable and hesitant to negotiate salaries. This has to change. It is part of the process for changing jobs and navigating corporate America. I still get nervous whenever I am negotiating a salary with a company I want to work for. The key is to tap into your personal board of directors to help you through this process. It essential to ensure that you are adequately being compensated for the value you bring to your organization.

Additionally, as employees of color, do not be concerned with your humble beginnings.

There are virtues you have gained from working your way up from the bottom. Most likely, you are more tenacious than your fellow competitors in the job market. If you've worked less than stellar jobs in your past, harness that grit and perseverance that once got you through those sluggish shifts. Your start in life does not determine your end.

LESSON 5.2: TREAT THE COMPANY LIKE YOU OWN IT

Whatever position you hold, you can be a steward of the company, its mission, its vision, and its resources. Even if it is stocking shelves at a beauty supply store. This is one of the fastest ways to gain credibility and trust from your executive team. Senior executives are always impressed with employees who go out of their way to deliver high-quality work with a sense of accountability and ownership. This is the type of employee executives can entrust with more responsibility. Set yourself apart from the crowd by stepping up to find creative ways to save the company money or increase efficiencies. Additionally, stepping up and showing leadership as a team member is one of the fastest ways to get promoted to manager. All an executive wants is someone who will make business-savvy decisions that add incremental value.

A true test of trust is who your boss puts in charge in their absence. They are likely to choose someone who thinks like they do and can be trusted unconditionally. A key sign that your boss or supervisor is beginning to trust you is how vulnerable they are with you. When they begin to share frustrations or pull away the veil of secrecy in any way, cherish these moments. Be present. Honor confidentiality. And be sure to reciprocate. That will nurture the budding relationship even more. If an executive can have a very real human moment with you, it is because they trust you. This could be the beginning of a relationship with your executive leader that can lead to amazing career opportunities in the future. It can be transformative.

CHAPTER 6

Make the Most of Your Mentor

The Right Mentor Makes All the Difference in the World

> A mentor is someone who allows you to see the higher part of
> yourself when sometimes it becomes hidden to your own view.
>
> —*Oprah Winfrey*

In corporate America, when you can connect a positive, hardworking attitude with the right mentors in your life, success will come. However, in my experience, many people of color do one without the other. For those who have a modicum of success in corporate America, their focus is usually on the degrees (and student loan debt) they have earned and their work ethic. This is their formula for success. After a host of failures and multiple attempts to seek higher employment and promotional opportunities, they become despondent and unsure of themselves. Soon, they retreat into doing the bare minimum just to get by.

The dejection you may feel from being in the same role for years is palpable and frustrating. It feels like you are running in place. New hires join your company with bigger titles and higher salaries, and you end up training them! I see this struggle in many of the people I mentor. This is pervasive in the workplace. However, in my humble opinion, these employees have not pursued the full career equation: hard work + education + networks = advancement (Figure 6.1).

One day, I began to mentor a Black employee named Edwin, who had a job at another health insurance company in its operations department. Edwin had been with the company for over 12 years. He was a Senior Claims Analyst and had become one of the principal experts on his company's claims system. Edwin was known as a hard worker and always took on the toughest assignments. You know, those tasks that no one else dares to do—the type of risky assignment that can be high profile but only leads to agony if it is not completed on time or under budget. Edwin leaned into those

HARD WORK + EDUCATION + NETWORKS =
ADVANCEMENT

Figure 6.1 The Full Career Equation: Hard Work + Education + Networks = Advancement

assignments and happily accepted the accompanying challenges. He had not pursued advanced education since he became a claims examiner out of high school. Back then, the job paid very well and beat working at a mall. Plus, the company hired him into an entry-level role where he trained for three months. At the time, Edwin thought to himself, who could beat the benefits, decent salary, and free training? Thus, he came onboard at the young age of 24 years old. Through the next 12 years, Edwin had three promotions and more than 15 different bosses. Now, he was 36 years old and had two children to raise and nurture.

Without ever saying it, Edwin felt like he hit a ceiling at work. What can be called a glass ceiling for women today in corporate America can feel like a *concrete ceiling* for people of color. You cannot even *see* the top. If you happen to be a person of color, a female, or both, the odds are stacked against you. During Edwin's tenure, he witnessed dozens of newly hired managers who knew way less than he did. Indeed, most of them relied on his expertise. Edwin thought to himself, *Why am I being ignored? What do I have to do to get to the next step?*

The reality is that Edwin was never eligible for a managerial position because this company, like the vast majority, strictly required a college degree or *requisite experience* for serious advancement—those tricky, nebulous words used by recruiters in HR departments that allow for abundant subjectivity in the selection process for new or current employees. Edwin sat in his corporate role for years, watching life and new employees with college degrees pass him by.

By the time we met and spoke about his advancement prospects, I told him about the full career equation and his eyes suddenly opened. For the past 12 years, his sole focus had been to be the best Senior Claims Analyst in the company. Unfortunately, this was not enough.

Do you know how that has been rewarded? I would ask him.

The answer: many more years of working as a claims analyst with no prospect of growth or advancement. I tried to share the employer's point of view with Edwin. "They know you're a hard-working employee who is really good at his job. From their desire to be efficient and improve output metrics, keeping you in that position at the lowest possible salary as long as possible is the end goal."

I tried to give him useful and actionable advice. Hard work is not enough to make it up the corporate ladder, let alone the corporate mountain that exists for people of color. You are receiving your paycheck and increase every year. From the employer's perspective, this transactional relationship is working perfectly.

Then we discussed education. He told me that since he had already been trained on the company system, he did not see what a degree would bring to the table. "How would it actually help?" Edwin also added that many of his previous managers were not as smart as their resumes would imply.

I agreed with him. College degrees do not prove intelligence. They do not even certify managerial capabilities. All that a college degree can present to a hiring manager is empirical evidence of someone's sticking to an arduous task for four or more years. A degree exemplifies perseverance, discipline, and achievement. The mere fact that someone pays tuition to invest in themselves is a clear sign that they have ambition to do more and learn more.

Often, people of color forgo education because they believe they already have the requisite skills that a degree will not enhance. Or they do not believe that the benefits of the degree will outweigh the potential for student debt. The most understated benefit of a degree, however, is the assurance of transferable skills. An academic degree is usually documented evidence that you can be a versatile player in the company and work on a variety of different projects supporting numerous departments.

While this may also be true if you're an employee without such a degree, you now place yourself at the mercy of the recruiter and hiring manager to value your experience against someone else's experience and education. Personally, I never wanted education to be a factor in my advancement. To take that off the table, I pursued bachelor's, master's, and doctoral degrees. I am not suggesting that everyone do this in order to advance their careers, but it is imperative to be aware of the abundant opportunities that present themselves with undergraduate and advanced degrees. And the probability you will never obtain a higher role in the company without one.

Edwin shot back that he knows vice presidents who lack college degrees. "Why does it matter?" Again, I agreed with him. This brought us to the third variable of the equation: networks. I asked him a slew of questions. *How well do you know your manager? How many children does she or he have? Where did they grow up? What is their alma mater? Their favorite sports team?* Then I asked how well he knew his manager's boss, posing similar questions. Was he a member of any groups or associations focused on managed care, claims, and/or professional development?

As Edwin and I spoke, he realized that because he prioritized hard work over everything else, he did not know his leadership team well. Of course, he knew some information about them, the type of details that are exchanged by co-workers during shared pleasantries in meetings. But all of his deeper relationships in the company were with other people of color—who were at the same level that he was in the organization, or lower.

There is a book by Dr. Beverly Daniel Tatum entitled *Why Are All the Black Kids Sitting Together in the Cafeteria?* In it, she describes that undeniable bond, sense of belonging, and solace that schoolchildren of color feel sitting next to one another. If they happen to attend a school where they are underrepresented, one way to affirm their identity is by sitting together. Well, we are creatures of habit. Our need to congregate with those similar to us surely occurs in the workplace as well.

Edwin spent his time forging really good, long-lasting relationships with his Black and Brown peers, none of whom could accelerate his career aspirations or advancement. Most organizations in America see diversity decrease the higher you move up. Employees of color have to get out of this comfort zone and learn to build networks with people who do not look like themselves. That is why building broadly diverse professional networks is so vital to your growth and advancement. Networks are interconnected groups of people who exchange information and ideas through professional relationships. Networks help you find out about positions in the company before they are ever posted online. Having connections to others who are in a position of power to help you is paramount to ascending the corporate mountain. Edwin needed to realize that his first managerial role would come about by a hiring manager taking a chance on him. It is nearly impossible to build such a level of trust with a hiring manager during the interview process. If you are not networking and building key relationships within the company, you are greatly limiting your chances of success.

Edwin also needed his own Sempai. Indeed, all of us marginalized employees in corporate America need as many mentors as we can muster. You need someone who can vouch for you, praise and promote you in the rooms you have yet to access. Having a great mentor is absolutely paramount for your professional and personal success.

Edwin seemed unaware about the importance of networks and mentorship, and recognized that his White peers had an easier time forging relationships with upper-level management than he did. Whether this notion is true is not debatable. It is a fact. Dr. Tatum would argue that it is also neurological science. Thus, once we are presented with this truth, it is our mission to strategize and overcome these barriers.

In my experience, employees of color have to operate at a higher level for a longer period of time before they become eligible for promotion. This is how the corporate world works. I have fired over 100 people in my 18-year career, but I have also promoted well over 200 people in that same period. Those I promoted were employees who grew out of their roles. They acted like managers even though they were still associates. They transformed their language from the individual "I" to the collective "we." They focused on how to advance the corporate goals and objectives rather than putting themselves first. If you can put your company first, your team second, and yourself last, you will be in the best position to climb the corporate mountain.

Mentors come in all shapes and sizes, but make no mistake, they can be an essential ingredient in your career success. If they are missing from your current career journey, it is time for you to pursue some mentors in your life. What are Mentors? They are trusted advisors who guide you through your life and career.

When Odysseus, the legendary king of Ithaca in Homer's epic Greek poem *The Odyssey*, left for the Trojan War, there was only one person he felt was principled and reliable enough to watch over his son, Telemachus, while he was away. That person was an older man by the name of Mentor. Mentor took Telemachus under his wing and imparted his wisdom as he stood in for Odysseus during his absence.

Similarly, when I was unsure of what to do with my first offer letter, I went to the person I trusted the most: my mentor, Greg. I knew he would only have my best interests at heart. It is not easy to find this type of relationship in a stranger. Mentors should be free from bias. I personally believe that your boss cannot adequately be your non-biased mentor. After all, you may want to complain about your boss to your mentor. You also want to hear feedback from your mentor about how to approach your boss. A mentor is a guide, with more knowledge than you, who selflessly provides you with the feedback you need to grow. Sometimes that advice might be tough to hear. My mentors gave me the courage to make a million mistakes and the wisdom to not make the same mistake a million

Bruce Jackson

Associate General Counsel and Managing Director, Strategic Partnership, Microsoft Author of Never Far from Home

"My first "mentor" was a maintenance guy at my elementary school. He opened the gym up for us to play so we wouldn't be on the street. I realize now that he could've lost his job if one of us got hurt. He wanted to get us kids off the street so we could play basketball all day. I think there's an obligation for all of us to reach down, when we do make it, to pull people up. I would advise people now that if you have any inkling about what it is you want to do, just reach out and try to set up a meeting and discuss your career path. Look at people who are successful and try to reach out to them. Or people like them. Don't just wait. If someone reaches a hand down, great. But if they don't, don't stop your dream waiting for that to happen. They don't necessarily have to be someone who looks like you. You want to have a broad perspective. The help that I received came from people from different ethnic groups and genders as well."

times. Finding a great mentor is hard; being a great mentee is even harder. You must select mentors wisely and come prepared to work.

LESSON 6.1: FIND THE RIGHT MENTOR

A well-managed mentoring relationship can transform your career. However, the hardest part of the process is finding the right mentor.

Here are few steps to take to finding the right mentor.

1. **Identify the problem.** Before thinking about who you should select as a mentor, first identify the problem or issue you are trying to solve. For example, if you are an introvert seeking to learn ways to improve your public speaking and networking skills, then the type of mentor you select will be different than if you are thinking about changing industries. Far too often, mentees select mentors based on their stature in the company or their public appeal on social media rather than finding that mentor who has the skill sets, experiences, and knowledge that will help mentees achieve their goals.

2. **Cast a wide net.** A common misconception about mentors is that they have to be a C-Suite executive or a senior leader in your industry. However, the best mentoring relationships sometimes come from colleagues who are just a few steps ahead of you in their own career. Why? It is likely that their advice will resonate with you more and have more of a practical application. Second, the best mentors are usually someone you gravitate toward because of their energy or the way they move through the world. Most of my mentors inspire me. Do not limit yourself by age, gender, race, or industry. Many of the mentors in my career were older White men with whom I had little in common. While these relationships were awkward at first, they grew over time to where our relationships have become so close that our bonds are unbreakable.

3. **Build a rapport.** It is important to build a professional relationship with someone be-fore you ask them to become a mentor. Far too often, I receive messages from strangers on LinkedIn asking me to mentor them. While I am flattered at the requests, it tells me that they are still in the incubation phase of forming their networks. It is okay to reach out to professionals on LinkedIn seeking professional growth op-portunities, but the first question should not be about mentorship. Build a rapport with your potential mentor first. Get to know a little bit about them with initial emails or phone calls. Based on these initial conversations, you may find that the person is not ideal for mentorship. A good starting point is consistent dialogue for roughly three to six months.

> **Denise J. Brown**
>
> *Entertainment Attorney and Former Senior Vice President of Warner Bros. Records Ordained Minister*
>
> "I've always had mentors, champions and allies. They came in all shapes and sizes: White men, Black men, and Black women. They have always encouraged me in my career, which was really helpful. In choosing a mentor, look for someone who's actually doing what it is you want to do. Don't be afraid to reach out to them and ask them to mentor you! I mean, most people are happy to do that."

4. **Make the ask.** You would not believe the number of employees of color I have spoken to throughout the years who are petrified about asking someone to be their mentor. The mentorship will never formalize between you and the other person until you are both on the same page about the relationship you want to build. Since you have built a rapport with this person for the past three to six months, making the ask should be a bit easier. By that time, you'll know if the mentorship will be fruitful. Assess how often they respond to

Kate Simpson

Client Account Manager, Big Five accounting firm

"To be a good mentee, I would say, come with an agenda. Don't just show up to the call and expect the other person to lead. Come with your questions. Ask them about themselves, their journeys. Come with something to offer. Be willing to give your time or research for them. This relationship works two ways. Not just one-directional. Come with something you know you can offer to support them. Ask them if they have any ideas they want to bounce off, but are afraid to do so. Volunteer for them to bounce it off you."

your emails or outreaches. How rich and inclusive are your conversations with them? Have you built up a rapport enough to where there is friendly banter and some vulnerability between the two of you? Soon, you'll have a sense of whether or not the relationship will work well. If you think it will, make the ask!

LESSON 6.2: BECOMING A MENTEE TAKES TIME

Now that you've successfully formalized a relationship with someone and officially have a mentor, what comes next?

While many leadership books focus on the importance of obtaining a mentor, few explain what is required to be a great mentee. There are roles and responsibilities of a mentee that will help to foster a strong and long-lasting relationship with your mentor. Being a proper mentee takes talent and tenacity. It also takes TIME:

TIME

- Trust
- Intentionality
- Milestones
- Evaluation

Here are the keys to success for being a great mentee:

- **Trust:** Above all, as a mentee you must foster trust. That means being accountable, dependable, and respectful of your mentor's time. Simple things like showing up on time for meetings instills trust and mutual respect with your mentor. A mentee must also ensure that their discussions remain private and confidential. As you build a rapport with your mentor, they may begin to share more with you. Trust between the two of you is cardinal. It can take years to build trust, but you can lose it in seconds if you are not careful.

- **Intentionality:** Work must be done to prepare for mentorship meetings. A one-hour mentorship meeting should take at least one hour of preparation time. Mentees must set the framework and scope for the mentor relationship. You must define in advance what your success and goals will look like and the duration of the mentoring relationship. You should also set the agenda for each mentor meeting and send it well in advance so the mentor can properly prepare. Remember, this special relationship is a two-way street. Don't forget to offer to help your mentor with any of their activities. Also, make sure to be open to candid feedback from the mentor to nourish this vital relationship. I once had a mentee ask me why we had not spoken in so long. My response was short and to the point: "Because you have not arranged any time." Give your mentoring relationship the time and respect it deserves. Have a reason for every interaction and make judicious use of your mentor's time.

Lucy M. Lopez

General Counsel and Chief Legal Officer at Spencer Stuart, a leading global executive search and leadership advisory firm

"You have to take stock of what you want from a mentor, being mindful not to be overly demanding of their time. Be thoughtful about when to reach out and how often, respecting their time and being prepared with your questions and ideas for discussion. You want your mentor to feel like they are making a difference and that their investment in you is impactful. And importantly, don't make it just about you. The success of your mentor should be as important to you as your success is to them."

- **Milestones:** Mentorships can be time-bound or bound by milestones. Set time-bound milestones with your mentor and make sure you are consistently focused on key issues or projects. For example, when I first became a vice president with more than 400 people reporting into my division, my mentor and I focused on my first 100 days. All of our conversations over the next three months were focused on coaching and advice around that topic. We scheduled regular meetings, but since we had built a rapport through the years, I could also text or call him when urgent issues arose. We even spoke on weekends as I prepared for significant Monday meetings with my executive leadership team. Milestones keep the relationship on track and allow you to celebrate your wins or analyze your failures.

- **Evaluation:** After some time with your mentor, it never hurts to set up an agenda item on evaluating your mentor/mentee relationship as a way to ensure that you are both getting the same value out of the relationship. It is also a way to determine whether both parties still have the bandwidth and/or desire to continue. Great mentorships can last a lifetime. However, not every mentoring relationship will last forever. Provide your mentor an opportunity to give you feedback on the relationship. Like any relationship, these relationships can wax and wane with changes in life. However, one thing is for certain, always keep in contact with your closest mentors. Send a holiday card to keep them updated on your life and your career. Wish them happy birthday. Check in on them with no other agenda item but to say hello and hear how they are doing. Maintain and nourish these relationships. The greatest honor someone can bestow upon you is the willingness to take a stake in your personal and professional success. Often, your closest mentors magically transform into your closest friends.

CHAPTER 7

Recognize and Harness Your Champions

Champions Are Larger-Than-Life People Who Give You a Boost

Show me a successful individual and I'll show you someone who had real positive influences in his or her life. I don't care what you do for a living—if you do it well, I'm sure there was someone cheering you on or showing the way.

—*Denzel Washington*

*M*ensch. It's a Yiddish word that means a person of integrity or honor.[1] I've heard the term a few times in my life, but I finally understood the true meaning after meeting a man named Donald L. Ashkenase. May he rest in peace. Don was a revered leader of the New York healthcare community for several decades. There was not a hospital executive around who did not know his name. Not a single healthcare executive had anything but kind and positive words to say about him. I would soon learn why.

Don graduated from Brooklyn College in 1965 and went on to serve four years in the U.S. Air Force as a hospital administrator. After serving his country, Don received his master's degree from Wagner College. He started his career at New York City Health and Hospitals Corporation, the largest American municipal healthcare system, today generating more than $7 billion in revenue. This hospital served the most vulnerable of New Yorkers—the homeless, poor, and destitute—those who simply could not afford quality health insurance. While there, he fortified his passion for serving the have-nots and became a vocal advocate for *health equity* many years before the term ever became popular.

After serving as Chief Financial Officer (CFO) of both New York City Health and Hospitals Corporation and the Long Island Jewish Medical Center, in 1987, Don would find himself working at the Montefiore Medical Center, a hospital in The Bronx, home to the 15th District, the poorest congressional district in the United States.[2] Ironically, Montefiore was named after another mensch, Sir Moses Haim Montefiore, a well-known and revered nineteenth-century British-Jewish businessman and philanthropist.

Thus, it seemed preordained that Don would work at Montefiore. For virtually the next quarter century, his responsibilities and status would grow and grow there. In 1993, Don became the board chairman of a small nonprofit health insurance company partially sponsored by Montefiore. Always a generous benefactor, Don gave back to his community in a myriad of ways. He would have made Sir Moses Montefiore very proud indeed.

Montefiore was where I had the great fortune to cross paths with Don, this bona fide mensch, when I decided to work at this small nonprofit health insurance company in 2012 while he was still the chairman of the board. It was Monday, September 24, 2012, to be exact. I remember it well because before I received a company-issued laptop, I was asked to give a presentation to the entire leadership team to explain the Affordable Care Act. Fortunately, I had read the entire bill, all 2,000-plus pages, as part of my graduate studies at New York University, where I was pursuing my Master's in Public Administration at the time. I was only 29 at the time. What I did not know was that I was one of the youngest Assistant Vice Presidents in the company—and one of the highest-ranking African Americans as well. I quickly understood that when I entered the meeting room. First impressions are everything. The powers-that-be can brand you in either a positive or negative light. I realized this and strived to always do my best. I still recall trying to somehow expel my butterflies so I would not feel them in my stomach while I spoke. I also was sure to project my voice as it was crucial to exude confidence.

The presentation went well. My boss congratulated me for speaking on such short notice. A few weeks later, I was asked by the COO to make a similar speech, but this time to the board. The Affordable Care Act was signed into law by President Barack Obama on Tuesday, March 23, 2010. By 2012, all health plans had to begin implementing the law, which would go into effect in 2014.

I remember joining the board meeting, the first one of my life. Even the term *board meeting* sounded intimidating. Entering a boardroom was equally scary. I recall how it felt to be in a room where I did not believe I belonged. The room was filled with mostly older White men, and I was easily 20 to 30 years their junior. When I entered, I deliberately did not make eye contact with them. I just lacked the confidence at the time. I was so uneasy; I did not know where to sit or put my hands, what to do, or where to go.

I stood and waited as board members began to file in and take their seats. As the room filled, I decided to take the most distant seat from the folks who seemed to be the most important in the room. Lunch was served, but I dared not venture to eat or drink. Why bring unneeded attention to myself? My boss came over to me and asked if I was ready. I nodded yes. But I was lying. I was not ready. *Ready for what?* I thought to myself.

As a person of color, I was anguished over how to act and what to do. *Do I tell my boss that I have never attended a board meeting?* Would my lack of experience be held against me? Would they regret their decision to hire me? My mind was spinning out of control. Rather than focusing on what I was going to say during my presentation, I was filled with worries about my acceptance in this room. I physically felt my self-esteem slip away.

Fortunately, my presentation was not first on the agenda. When the meeting was called to order, I was able to witness the board procedures and memorize the gestures and jargon of the board—that, perhaps, I could later utilize or mimic.

"Next on our agenda is a business update. This discussion will focus on the Affordable Care Act legislation. To speak to it in detail is Errol Pierre, our new Assistant Vice President of product management," uttered my COO. The entire room stared at me. *Me. This short, young, Black kid with razor bumps living in The Bronx.* Too often, people of color psych themselves out, way before anyone else gets a chance to. Before even thinking about the response of these board members, I was already consumed with negative thoughts about myself. This habit can exponentially set employees of color back because we can easily become our own worst enemies. Ambition and advancement are already hard enough as we climb this corporate mountain; there is no need for self-sabotage as well. We are sure to encounter enough hate on our journeys without hating ourselves to boot.

I powered through the presentation. After concluding, I answered a variety of questions, as the board members began to discuss how complicated this law would be to implement and the unintended consequences of the policy. As the conversation came to a close, the

Chairman of the Board spoke up. When he started to speak, everyone went quiet.

The Chairman thanked me for my presentation. He complimented me on how well I spoke and acknowledged my command of the new legislation. The chairman also expressed his confidence in the company's leadership to eventually implement the new law. The meeting soon ended and we adjourned. Mr. Ashkenase then made his way to me. He was a short, older man with silver-gray hair. Despite his diminished stature, he commanded serious respect throughout the hallways of the office and, of course, within the four walls of our boardroom.

Don Ashkenase stuck out his hand and said, "What an amazing presentation. You understand the details so well. This Act is not easy to implement, but you answered every question. Young man, this company is lucky to have you. Keep up the great work." Suddenly, all of my anxiety, nervousness, and self-doubt melted away. The chairman had made it a point to acknowledge me. To see and meet me. To recognize my talents, knowledge, and indeed, my humanity. I'll never forget that feeling. In those precious moments, I was formally introduced to someone who would soon become the second champion of my life. Suzy, the COO of my former health insurance company, was my first. The earth had somehow conspired in my favor.

How did Don help me as a champion? From that moment on, he actively advocated for me and my professional pursuits. He spoke to my boss and my CEO about me. He became actively interested and supportive of my career and professional development. When Don was in our offices for board meetings and other matters of governance, he would always make it a point to stop by my office.

The first time he asked about me, my administrative assistant was startled! I was in a meeting and she did not know whether to (a) run and pull me out of the meeting; (b) pass me a note letting me know the chairman of the board wanted to see me; or (c) send me a personal text message. She ended up doing all three! My assistant was not the only one who was surprised. I was blown away! I couldn't believe Don wanted to visit me.

I remember being on a different floor and briskly jogging back to my office to see what the chairman required. When I arrived out of breath, Don simply smiled and greeted me. Then he asked me about my career, if I was advancing successfully and how he could help. Again, I was shocked. I told him I was very content with my job and my level of responsibility. Although this was the truth, Don always seemed to be impatient with my career advancement—more so than me! It was as if he wanted me to succeed more than I did, as if he saw my potential more clearly than I. Hell, at the time, I was just happy that my office building ID badge worked each day I walked in.

Don taught me to dream big and be persistent. He forced me to think about my career aspirations continually and produced a healthy tension between where I was and where he believed I could be.

"When are you going to be a vice president, Errol?" he asked me from time to time during our visits.

How would I know? I never knew how to answer these questions. I would politely say I was working on it. He would also let me know when he mentioned my name to my superiors. In the back of my mind, I always worried if they would think that *I* was the one asking Don to do this on my behalf. I wanted to scream to everyone that it wasn't me. That's how self-conscious I felt at the time. But our rapport continued to grow.

A few months passed, and magically I ended up back on the board agenda. This time, I was less nervous, more assertive, and definitely ready to make more eye contact. It was ironic that I had such a good rapport with the chairman, who grinned when I entered the room. His very warm smile intimated that he might have had something to do with me being there. This time, I confidently introduced myself to other board members. When it was time for my agenda item, I once again presented the update comprehensively. Don again complimented my presentation and me, and we then conversed about other topics.

Our relationship continued to build throughout the years. It grew so much that he asked me to guest lecture at his graduate school class. Don Ashkenase was a professor at Columbia University's School of Public Health. He taught a Transformational Healthcare Economics course in the Executive Master's in Health Administration program. Once again, he saw talents in me that I did not. In my mind, I had no business *teaching* in an Ivy League classroom. After all, these were mature students who had much more healthcare professional experience than I did. Of course, they would be much smarter and more talented than I was. I was sure of it. But Don assuaged my fears and encouraged me to give yet another presentation about the Affordable Care Act. Once again, I found myself in an unfamiliar setting doing something I never thought I could do. I now continue his legacy by teaching his class as a Columbia University faculty member and get to tell all of my students about Don. Don always made me punch above my weight class (Figure 7.1).

I remember an intimate moment we shared after teaching one of his classes. After all the students had left and it was just the two of us, Don grabbed my hands and said, "Errol, I was there at the March on Washington with Martin Luther King in 1964. You, Errol, you! You are the reason I was there. You are the reason Martin Luther King was marching. You are amazing." Full of emotions, I was rendered speechless. I tried to reply but could not. To me, my champion Don was the one who was amazing, even magical. An angel on Earth. He was also a visionary and ahead of his time, clearly the crown jewel of the

Figure 7.1   After guest lecture in Don Ashkenase's class, December 18, 2016.

healthcare industry in New York. And I got to call him a friend and, most importantly, my champion. Champions can change your life. Don certainly changed mine. But he also taught me the truest definition of the word mensch.

LESSON 7.1: CHAMPIONS ARE NOT MENTORS

Don was not my mentor, and I was not his mentee. He was not an advisor or a guide who helped me on an everyday basis to navigate daily roadblocks. Rather he was a supportive champion. A sponsor. In an April 2021, *Harvard Business Review* article, Cindy Gallop and Tomas Chamorro-Premuzic define a champion in this way: "A champion is someone who makes things happen for you. Someone who is prepared to go out on a limb for you. A champion is someone who, behind closed doors, slams their fist on the boardroom table and says, 'If there's only room for one bonus in the budget, it's going to Jane, not John.' In other words, a champion is a committed sponsor who has the agency to influence people at the top and will use it to help you, someone who will be your loyal brand ambassador and push for you to get ahead—even if it means jeopardizing their reputation by disrupting the status quo."[3]

What are champions? Tony's dad and Suzy the COO were my champions.

They did not work with me directly, but they placed me in a position to succeed and grow. You may not always have direct contact with your champions. You may not even know who they are. These are people who inherently see something in you and use their influence to fight on your behalf. Champions often work many levels above you. Champions talk about you in the rooms you have yet to be invited to. That's how glass and concrete ceilings get shattered: when champions advocate for diverse talent.

Champions are people who can drop a pebble in the water, but you can feel the ripples miles away. That is the power and influence they wield. When they are behind you, you are indeed blessed. Buckle up, and ride the wave to your advantage. But always remain humble.

LESSON 7.2: EMBRACE THE DISCOMFORT OF ACCEPTING HELP FROM AFAR

Sometimes champions will make themselves known to you. Sometimes they won't. They will be someone larger than life who takes time out of their day to acknowledge your existence. Do not push them away. When you receive attention in a corporate setting from someone so far up, take advantage of it. These opportunities come few and far between. Once you recognize them, begin to harness the relationship. Periodically send your champion updates about your career journey, but don't go into too many details. Keep it high level and specific to you and your career. They are aware of your talents but are less likely to intervene on your behalf on a day-to-day basis. They want you to learn on your own. It's important to use them wisely.

It took me a while to be comfortable with Don's help from afar. I felt that it gave me an unfair advantage in the workplace. While I appreciated his support, I always felt like I was cheating in a way. Do not think of the help you are receiving in this way, especially as a person of color. Corporate America needs *more* champions in high places advocating for the advancement of underrepresented employees. Sometimes, we in society confuse equity with equality. If we simply equally provide mentors and champions to everyone, our diversity statistics will remain the same. Equity seeks to undo the disparities that exist in corporate America. To shrink those gaps, corporate America will need

Stanley E. Grayson

Board Member of TD Bank, N.A. and Mutual of America Investment Corporation

"I think later in life, and certainly in my roles as a member of several corporate boards of directors, I have a keen appreciation of the notion of championing. . . . We each have a special mission when it comes to engaging and supporting those who look like us. I don't have any qualms about articulating that in the boardroom or outside of the boardroom. . . . All you can do is create the opportunity for exposure and advocate on someone's behalf where it makes sense. You do want to make sure that your colleagues know and understand that."

interventions that acutely increase the opportunities afforded to diverse employees.

When I think about the two champions in my life, Don and Suzy, the one thing I realize is this: I did not start at the same place on this planet as my White peers. Since it was harder for a Black kid living in The Bronx to acquire an ally in a corporate setting, a champion like Don was leveling the playing field for me. This is exactly what equity looks like.

This type of boost did not mean I was any less qualified for the roles or opportunities I received. In fact, I still had to perform *better* than my peers to stay in those roles. Even though Don opened doors for me, it was my responsibility to walk through them and be successful. Upon reflection, I probably underutilized my champions because of my self-consciousness and self-doubt. It was a mistake that I will not repeat again if I am fortunate enough to ever have another champion in my life.

LESSON 7.3: CHAMPIONS COME IN ALL SHAPES AND SIZES

You will probably have no more than three champions in your life. Both of mine were White people who supported my growth. One was Irish, and the other was Jewish. There was a large age difference between them and me. I had very little in common with either of them. I still have no idea why they took time to get to know me or why they risked their political capital on my behalf. However, the thing with champions is, you do not need to know why. They have their reasons.

Embrace the help from afar. Get over your discomfort from receiving their help. Focus on making them proud. Take full advantage of the doors they open for you. Realize that they are risking a bit of themselves on your behalf. Do not take that lightly. As you navigate your workplace, you are representing them. They have invested so much into you and your career. The best way to thank them is by living up to their expectations and making them proud.

A later chapter of this book, "Leading While Leaving a Legacy," discusses how when you reach the pinnacle of your career, the rule of thumb is to *Pay It Forward*. Both of my champions saw something in me and wanted to help me succeed. They were paying it forward because they also had champions in their life. Remember to move at your champion's pace and try not to be pushy or annoying. Always understand that your champion owes you nothing. If their support stops for whatever reason, be happy and grateful that they were in your life. I never officially called Don or Suzy my champions to their faces. But in retrospect, that's what they were. And I am forever grateful for it.

CHAPTER 8

Overcome the Entry-Level Blues

What to Do When You Feel Like You're Running in Place

I'm sick of us having to be perfect to get the job.
—*John Thompson, late Hall of Fame basketball coach of the Georgetown Hoyas and the first African American to lead his team to the NCAA championship*

You just landed your first official corporate job. Congratulations! *Now what?* I was confused after I landed my first position. When beginning your career, it is important to think about your endpoint first and be intentional about your professional development and progression. Of course, it is also crucial to allow yourself some flexibility in deciding where you want to be in 5 or 10 years. But once you decide, create a vision for your career and take action!

I bring this up because I have had junior members on my team who did not quite have a vision for their career. This often led them to making many professional decisions that lacked alignment and cohesion. One of those team members was Monica. She was a local student of color, born and raised in New York City. When she joined my product development team, it was her first job out of college. I always made myself available to such new hires, especially the ones right out of school. In the few times we spoke, I learned that she was really focused on becoming a manager. After 10 months in her new position, she scheduled a one-on-one meeting with me. On the day of the meeting, she walked into my office, sat down, and asked me how to move up to the next level in our company. I asked her *why* she wanted to become a manager and invited her to share what the next four to five years of her career could look like. My questions were met with silence. Monica was so focused on obtaining a higher title that she neglected to have any of the other more important details mapped out.

"It is easy to become a manager. It is much harder to figure out what type of manager you want to be," I explained. She asked for further information to better understand me.

That is when I pulled out a piece of paper and drew a big box. I then added lines within the box to create four horizontal columns and four vertical rows. I labeled three of the columns: INDIVIDUAL CONTRIBUTOR, MATRIXED LEADER, and PEOPLE LEADER. Then I labeled three of the rows: STRATEGIC, OPERATIONAL,

	Individual Contributor	Matrixed Leader	People Leader
Strategic			
Operational			
Technical			

Figure 8.1   Career Assessment Grid

and TECHNICAL. I was drawing for her something I call the Career Assessment Grid (Figure 8.1).

There were nine empty boxes in the middle that we began to fill with job titles as we continued our dialogue.

I posed a question to her. "Monica, which box do you want to be in?"

She looked at me inquisitively and said, "I don't know, Errol."

That's when I further explained the grid and what each box means. When thinking about how and why you want to grow in an organization, it is best to think about the activities you want to be involved in everyday work life. This is much more important than simply the title of the position you seek. Focusing on the activities that resonate with you first will clarify which path to pursue. The job title comes last in the equation.

For example, some team members love to do independent work and are ideal virtual or remote employees. They enjoy analytical work they can process on their computer but do not really enjoy meetings and speaking to other team members. These individuals are definitely Individual Contributors who serve a valuable purpose in a company.

I also have members of my team who are the exact opposite. Their energy is derived from interacting with other team members. If they open up their Microsoft Outlook calendar and see a day of back-to-back meetings, it actually energizes them. That is, they look forward to the discussions and conversations that will follow. These individuals can either become future Matrixed Leaders or People Leaders.

The question to ask these social employees is if they also like to assume team responsibility and accountability. If they do, and the thought of coaching, disciplining, and managing teams sounds rewarding, then they definitely qualify as potential People Leaders. However, this is not for everyone. Some members on the team enjoy interacting with other employees, but feel that managing a team is an added burden that takes the enjoyment out of their work. These people tend to be Matrixed Leaders, and I have worked with plenty of them. These are individuals who enjoy leading projects and key initiatives for the company, but prefer not to handle the day-to-day people management required to do so.

Matrixed Leaders lead initiatives that cross many different departments and drive teams to certain outcomes and delivery dates. However, in some instances, they do not have to worry about approving paid time off, handling employee disputes, or hiring and firing large groups of colleagues. Matrixed managers tend to have a handful of direct reports. They rarely have to provide regular coaching or performance reviews to large teams. They tend to not have a staffing budget. These are definitely parts of the job for People Leaders.

Matrixed Leaders often have the influence to get things done at a company even though the team members doing the work do not report to them directly. This is a form of "dotted line leadership" where the people on the team have their own boss, but for the purpose of the project, they are following the guidance and expectations of their Matrixed Leader; hence the term "matrixed." The three terms we discussed describe the columns at the top of the boxes in the chart. They focus on your identity or *who you want to be* in an organization.

Now the rows explain *what work you actually do* every day: "Strategic," "Operational," and "Technical." Strategic describes those employees who are focused on planning for their organization's future. They are corporate chess players, if you will. Much of the time, these strategic team members are thinking one to three years out or more. They are aware of the competitive environment, the latest products and services being offered in their market, and have a vision for the future.

An example of a role that is strategic and an individual contributor is Chief of Staff. I was the Chief of Staff to the President and CEO of the largest health insurance company in New York. In that role, 90% of the time I was focused on strategic planning and executing our organizational goals. However, I did not have any team members reporting to me. While I interacted with many members of the leadership team, I was not leading initiatives either. Thus, I served my President and CEO as an Individual Contributor.

Strategic roles with Matrixed Leaders include Project Leaders or Executive Directors within an organization. Project leaders are held accountable for the successful completion of companywide initiatives. They are charged with leading a team that has been assigned to them. However, these team members also have a day-to-day supervisor. While the Project Leader leads the project, our team members only report to them for the sole purpose of the project's completion. These types of roles are not easy to fill. Project leaders take on all of the accountability but have zero direct leadership over their team members. Success is dependent on their emotional intelligence and ability to get the most out of their team members.

Strategic People Leaders are individuals like the Chief Executive Officer or the profit/loss leader of an organization. These leaders tend to run very big teams and focus on coalescing various parts of the organization to achieve specific cross-functional goals. They provide vision, create the environment most conducive to success, and set the strategic priorities for an organization. Strategy can happen in multiple parts of the organization, especially in Operations, Marketing, and Information Technology. It heavily relies on the industry or how the organization is set up. However, this rubric is most commonly seen in big organizations.

Operational roles describe those jobs that focus on performance, efficiency, and reliability. Operations focus on metrics and efficiencies that ensure the effective use of a company's resources. In short, they make things happen. Operational teams fill the gap between a plan and the execution of that plan.

Individual Contributors in operational roles tend to be auditors or employees focused on quality control. They work independently but focus on metrics and overall performance impacting the firm. They can also be line staff in a production shop, similar to call center representatives or an employee on a factory line. A Matrixed Leader in operations could be a product owner or program director leading an operational implementation of a new platform or technological capability. Additionally, if policies or procedures need to be adjusted for a particular operational area, like a call center, leaders in an operational role can bring that to fruition. Operational leaders tend to be very focused on daily, monthly, and quarterly targets. They search for ways to improve speeds without sacrificing quality. People Leaders in these operational roles can be a Chief Operating Officer, Head of Operations, or Vice President of customer service.

P.S. Perkins

Human Communication Practitioner; Author of The Art and Science of Communication

"Our technology and our futuristic ways of looking at life and living have far out-distanced our ability to love one another, get along with one another, respect and honor the sameness of who all we are."

Lastly, there are technical roles in an organization. Technical leaders build the tools and capabilities for which organizational work gets done. For example, with the advent of the Coronavirus Pandemic in early 2020, it was up to the technical teams to figure out how to seamlessly migrate at-work employees to virtual employees. They made sure teams continued working despite being isolated from one another. Technical teams select the technology that will best assist strategic and operational teams in achieving their goals and meeting their business demands. As digital technology becomes paramount in many different industries, technology teams are becoming a larger part of the strategic conversations, and even leading them!

Individual Contributors in technical roles are business analysts, developers, or coders, as well as software engineers. Matrixed Leaders in technical roles can be product owners or system engineering managers. People leaders in the technical space can be IT Directors or Chief Information Officers (CIOs).

In simple terms, think of an organization as a car. Strategic people focus on the destination as well as the best route to get there. Operational teams will scrutinize the miles per gallon in order to maximize fuel efficiency. They will also make sure the car maintenance is up to date (e.g., air in the tires, timely oil changes). Technical teams will decide which GPS system should be used for the journey and, for example, the best tires to use that time of the year based on the distance of the trip.

It is important to have this kind of matrix in the back of your mind when deciding how to build your career. You need to understand what roles you should pursue so they are aligned with your long-term career aspirations. Once I walked my junior team member, Monica, through these various options, she understood her future career trajectory with much more clarity.

"I think I am a matrixed leader who can sit between operational and strategic roles," she said excitedly (Figure 8.2).

Timothy S. Taylor

Former Senior Counsel of the New York State United Teachers Union

"There are still things I want to accomplish going forward, and you should always have goals at every point in your life. Up to your dying day, you should have goals. You should write those goals down every day."

All entry-level employees should take on this level of focus for their future goals. Every career decision they make influences their

	Individual Contributor	Matrixed Leader	People Leader
Strategic	Chief of Staff	Project Leader	Chief Executive Officer
Operational	Auditor Call Center Agent	Program Director	Chief Operating Officer Head of Operations
Technical	Business Analyst Software Engineer	Product Owner	Chief Information Officer VP, App Development

Figure 8.2   Career Assessment Grid (Completed)

future success. The projects you choose and the positions you apply for should align with where you want to go in the company. I have met too many entry-level employees of color who have changed roles without intention and now have a resume with three to five years of experience that lacks cohesion; it is all over the place. Their experience simply does not hang together or align. It is hard to get a read on their focus. Are they changing roles for the wrong reasons? Or do they lack focus altogether?

As employees of color, our career choices may be even more important. We also have to be aware of the dichotomy that exists for us in corporate America. There is a difference between how people of color perceive themselves compared with how the world perceives them. This is a concept called *double consciousness*, coined by famed author, sociologist, historian, and civil rights pioneer W. E. B. Du Bois in a piece called "Of Our Spiritual Strivings" from his 1903 book *The Souls of Black Folk*. Du Bois explains, "One ever feels his twoness, an American, a Negro; two souls, two thoughts, two unreconciled strivings; two warring ideals in one dark body, whose dogged strength alone keeps it from being torn asunder."[1]

Sachin H. Jain, MD, MBA

Recognized by Modern Healthcare *magazine as one of American healthcare's 100 most influential leaders*

"I think minority leaders have to simultaneously manage two conflicting identities. One is the identity of the executive in the role that you've been granted. And the second is in the identity of a person of color in that role and trying to drive change. I think about this as being the problem that Obama faced when he was president. He simultaneously needed credibility as the president, but he also needed to be the Black president. On a much smaller scale, it's something we all face every day when you're a leader of color. You're not only a CEO, but you're also an Indian American CEO. You have to bear the simultaneous weight of the job, but also of being a representative of a community."

I have personally come face to face with double consciousness in the workplace. It required me to prove myself in order to overcome the institutional bias of perception before I even had a chance to perform! This does not always happen with malicious intent. Often, it can originate from the implicit biases many of us possess. *Implicit Bias* is a subconscious bias that can impact internal company decisions. These are difficult to acknowledge and address since they are subtle, and we are generally uncomfortable dealing with these types of issues in the workplace. Indeed, we have not been taught the language to address bias in the workplace. Claims of bias can often lead to challenging someone's character, which becomes personal if not confrontational.

There are three truths that I know in my heart:

1. Good people can have bad biases.

2. Well-intentioned people can unconsciously act on those biases.

3. We all have biases, regardless of our race, ethnicity, or gender.

The more we understand bias, the more we can try to eradicate it when it appears. (I return to this in Chapter 14.)

It behooves us to address accusations of bias head-on. We must not put the feelings and egos of the bias perpetrators above those of the victims. Unfortunately, I have witnessed this way too much in the workplace.

I often feel like there is an implicit caste system in America. As an affluent, well-educated person of color, I have access to places and people that many others do not. I am also treated differently by others once my socioeconomic class is revealed. For example, when I think about how I am treated as a Black man in the coach section on an airplane as compared to first class, the difference is night and day. The tone, language, and level of respect I receive in first class is so starkly different from that at the back of the plane.

Unfortunately, this social class structure also exists in the workplace. As you move up in corporate America, you will be treated differently. As you advance, you will also be rewarded for maintaining the

Timothy S. Taylor

Former Senior Counsel of the New York State United Teachers Union

"Start with the end in mind. Know what you're going to need when you get where you want to go.

If you're not getting opportunities for advancement, you can look around and start to create the opportunities that you don't think you're getting. Go to the Managing Partner and ask why you're not getting the golden nuggets. Don't be afraid to ask this question. Once they tell you why, go look in the mirror; figure out if what they're saying is true. If it is, make the necessary adjustments. But never rely on somebody else for your success. If you don't like where you are, you have an obligation to yourself to develop your own client base, your own opportunities in the world. . . . If you think you're that talented, do your own thing. If you think you should be flying the brand-new 747 and your company is not letting you, then go work for a different airline. Or build your own damn plane."

status quo. The question will be if you can acknowledge your privilege as a person of color while fighting for your colleagues who are not as fortunate as you. Career conversations like the one I had with Monica cannot flourish with bias lingering around an organization. The objective is to pursue growth opportunities with an end goal in mind, being fully aware of the biases you'll have to navigate along the way.

But what can you do if you feel left out? I once mentored Lisa, a Black woman in a leadership position, who had a boss who never initiated any interactions with her. Their one-on-one meetings seemed to always be as brief as possible. Her attempts to make small talk were met with curt responses. Despite her best efforts at networking, she never seemed to belong to the in-crowd. I remember her describing the most awkward and depressing feeling of walking through the office and seeing all of her boss's direct reports in a meeting except for her. Whether she was intentionally left off the list or just neglected, it hurt. She had to walk back to her office in a different direction to avoid passing the conference room again. She simply did not want to be seen by them.

When you feel ostracized, you feel like you are doing something wrong, but have no idea what it is. Corporate cultures can easily sustain an environment of passive aggression. You know something is off, but no one tells you what it is. Without direct information, you soon begin to imagine what it might be and your mind goes into a thousand different directions. This mental anguish can be distracting and knock you off your game. You can also lose confidence in yourself.

Lisa became more despondent in the office and spoke less with others. It can be debilitating to be in this situation, particularly if you don't know why. If you feel left out, and this behavior continue or worsens, you must do something!

One of the first responses to combat these experiences naturally is to change who you are in an attempt to fit in. This has been called *Code-Switching*. A recent article from the *Harvard Business Review* states that code-switching "involves adjusting one's style of speech, appearance, behavior, and expression in ways that will optimize the comfort of others in exchange for fair treatment, quality service, and employment opportunities."[2]

An example of code-switching is when people of color emulate the people and the culture with whom they work with in an effort to fit in. In doing so, they become inauthentic people who have the burden of managing two different personalities and worldviews. I have code-switched in my career to move ahead. I still code-switch, although now I believe I do it unconsciously. It usually shows up in the words I use. Occasionally, I laugh at jokes that make social references beyond my sphere of influence.

I remember one of my peers at work made a joke in reference to the 1950s show *The Adventures of Ozzie and Harriet*, saying I reminded him of the character Thorny by attempting to provide useless advice. I laughed out loud at the joke, while soon Googling the reference on my smartphone so I could understand it. The sheer act of laughing made me fit in at that moment.

My clothes and wardrobe are also part of code-switching. I'll never forget the time I left work after 6 p.m. and headed to the gym. After an hour-long workout, I walked to the subway to take the train

Indira Hector

Global HR Leader, AstraZeneca

"The thing about code-switching in the workplace is that what you're learning is White middle-class habits. As soon as you can't display those same habits, you're judged very quickly and subtly. You won't even know it. Maybe there's some word that you pronounce differently than they do or there is some joke that you made that they wouldn't have made. Even though it's not a bad joke, it may not be their thing. I think that you should be very aware of White middle-class norms to be successful in corporate America. I don't know if it's right or wrong. Sometimes you can educate people on different cultural norms. What I would like to see more of is also White males and White females being more curious about other cultural norms. They're the ones that need to learn, because I know White norms and White habits very, very well. They need to learn the norms of other people. They are the ones that need to learn how to code-switch."

home. As I entered the subway car, I recognized Kathryn, one of my senior executives. Excited, I walked up to her.

"Hi there!" I said enthusiastically.

Kathryn did not move. Her eyes stayed straight ahead. Her body did not lean toward my voice. We stood there for almost 30 seconds and then I just walked away. Mortified, I became uncertain it was her. Before I retreated to another subway car, I looked back and reaffirmed that she was indeed Kathryn. Embarrassed by what just transpired, I finally realized: I was in my gym clothes. I had just said hello to one of my executives in sneakers, jogging pants, and a hoodie, with earbuds. No wonder she didn't respond. I couldn't help but think that I most likely came across as a random guy asking for money. But since I was so close to the office, I didn't even consider my outfit because I'm usually dressed up in a shirt and tie. I didn't mention that encounter the next time I saw Kathryn, but had to continue working with her like nothing happened. Yet, another eggshell was placed at my feet to walk on gingerly.

Even when corporate events allow casual dress, I still tend to dress on the formal side of things. Overdressing is a safe habit for me because I know the perceptions that people have for an underdressed

Black male. Upon first impressions, we're rarely given the benefit of the doubt. If we're in the room, we must be "the help": a technician, janitor, security guy, or some other blue-collar worker. In college, I got arrested by police for simply fitting a description. I've since made a promise to myself to do everything in my power to never let this happen again.

I have mentored several employees of color, like Aditi, who struggled with navigating the office as an immigrant with a heavy foreign accent. Aditi felt the pressure to speak up, network, and share her ideas to get noticed by her boss. But she had a strong reluctance because she had faced discriminatory treatment due to her accent. Unfortunately, society can make assumptions about your intelligence based on your accent. But if Aditi remained silent, it would be hard for her to advance. I remember meeting with her monthly, and encouraging her to use her voice in meetings despite her accent. We also worked on prepping for meetings and doing practice runs. Whenever she was going to present, I encouraged her to write down her talking points and practice while looking in the mirror. This would boost her confidence so that when it came time to present, she was not as self-conscious about how she sounded. Aditi could instead be *present* in the meeting and participate.

Sachin H. Jain, MD, MBA

Recognized by Modern Healthcare *magazine as one of American healthcare's 100 most influential leaders*

"There was a meeting when we were kicking off this transformation. The meeting was being led by some really accomplished consultants from a major consulting firm. One of the leaders within the company came in a little bit late and asked another leader, "How's it going?" The leader said, " I can't understand a damn thing with these accents." They were all speaking perfect English. These consultants were senior partners at McKinsey and advise Heads of State and CEOs. I'll also just say there is an "old boys club" or people who know each other. People who know each other tend to look out for each other. If you're a minority in one of these big organizations and you don't have these people looking out for you, I think you end up sometimes being on the wrong end of things."

Social exclusion can happen to anyone in a company or organization. It can stem from a variety of sources that could be based on bias or on social cliques that form around a charismatic leader. It's important to take the necessary steps to rectify the situation.

LESSON 8.1: VOLUNTEER FOR PROJECTS

Once you've figured out where you want to end up on the Career Assessment Grid, start to volunteer for projects and initiatives outside the scope of your normal responsibilities. In the same way, if you are seeking a managerial position, identify yourself to our boss as someone who can be a team captain for specific projects with your team. The goal is to continuously amass experiences that will make your resume more robust. This is also a great way to differentiate yourself, showcase your leadership skills, and align yourself with your leadership team.

While you are putting forth all these efforts seeking new opportunities, do not lose momentum if you do not see immediate impact. I tell my mentees it can take 10 "no's" before you receive your first "yes." Imagine if you quit after your ninth no. And depending on the role, it might take 100 "no's." Do you have the stamina and the patience to fight through the first 99?

People of color can enter the workforce with social and cultural differences that can limit their exposure and connection to the higher-ups. They don't watch the same television shows, take the same summer vacations, or even eat the same foods. All the small talk that occurs in the office or on Zoom calls can sometimes make you feel left out of the conversation.

Code-Switching is one coping tactic. However, I have personally felt the negative toll this can take on the human mind, body, and soul. Code-Switching can become psychological warfare, especially if it leads to your success. You may wake up one day and realize that everyone at work who loves you doesn't really know the *real* you. This is something I often address in therapy as I strive every day to be the highest form of my authentic self.

When I was first starting out in my career, I once raised my hand to join a committee studying broker compensation across the country. By representing New York State on this project, I now had direct access to the plan president in a Midwestern state despite my being an entry-level product specialist. He was able to see my talents and work ethic firsthand. I was no longer dependent on my supervisor to expose me to senior executives—which is crucial to success.

Years later, when the plan president became the President and CEO of the company and interviewed me to become his Chief Operating Officer, he reminded me about our joint project from the past. To my great surprise and delight, he seemed genuinely impressed with what he saw in me all those years ago. This was indeed a chief catalyst to landing my first C-Suite position.

Had I decided not to raise my hand for that project many moons ago, or avoided networking with him throughout the duration of the project, I would have never left a lasting memory of myself in his mind. Just remember, sometimes it can take years to see the fruits of your labor.

Lesson 8.2: Beware the Consequences of Code-Switching

While you may feel the urge or social pressure to code-switch, be aware of the potential consequences. The price to fit in and feel part of a team is too high if you are required to be someone other than yourself. Remember, you are not the problem. There is

Indira Hector

Global HR Leader, AstraZeneca

"Most companies throw around the word inclusion a lot, but they don't have any real definition of it that people can understand. If you go to their corporate website, they have a definition, but if you take the average employee aside and say, "What is the definition of inclusion?," they cannot recite it back to you. How are employees practicing it every day if they don't know what it is? Actually, there are usually no tangible actions in these definitions. If they don't have any guidance or any specific behaviors that they're requiring, then most likely inclusion is not happening in a consistent way."

something inherently wrong with internal company cliques. In a professional setting, the goal is to build an environment of inclusion and belonging. If you do feel excluded, that reflects flawed leadership, not a judgment of you in any way. That being said, the powers that be cannot fix an issue if they don't know about it. Far too often, employees of color suffer in silence and in fear. There is an alternative. You just have to be strategic in how you try to change the culture at your workplace. I will share several strategies. However, before you enact such strategies, be self-reflective. Make certain that you are not doing anything that is causing you to shy away from your team.

Kate Simpson

Client Account Manager, Big Five accounting firm

"A lot of business happens after 5 p.m., so you just have to really go to the happy hour or Zoom equivalent because connections you make after office hours will result in opportunities. I started going to dinners and events, and I was able just to have small talk with colleagues. I was very surprised that, wow, these people can actually be your friends outside of work."

For example, if happy hour get-togethers are popular for your team members and you never go to them, it could appear that *you* are the one distancing yourself from the team and not the other way around. As people of color, we often shy away from these types of activities. However, these are the very activities that allow us to bond with our peers. Ask yourself if you are doing anything to give off the vibe that you do not want to socialize with your fellow team members.

Once you have assessed the situation and realize that the issue is them and not you, here is a step you can take.

Take an active approach in the topics and discussions brought up by your team. It is always good practice to assume good intent when you try to go about changing hearts and minds. What is the show that they talk about all the time? What is the common small talk topics around the water cooler or when the Zoom meetings start? When people discuss their weekends, what are their general themes? How much do you share? Are you as vulnerable as they are, or do you clam up and keep quiet?

Early in my career, I was intimidated by my senior executives. I believed them to be the smartest people at the company. How else had they obtained their positions? I had this fear that if I spoke up, they would discover how unintelligent and incompetent I was. As discussed earlier, I then realized this stemmed from impostor syndrome. In fact, a 2020 report from the International Socioeconomics Laboratory found that impostor syndrome impacts high-achieving BIPOC (Black, Indigenous, and People of Color) students, especially women, more than White students.[3] This feeling can prevent you from simply feeling normal when you go to work. I long to feel what it is to just be yourself and not have to worry about what people are thinking about you every second of the day. These insecurities can cloud your mind and knock you off your game. I won't say I have overcome my impostor syndrome, but rather I've learned to live with it. I keep a running list of my accomplishments and refer to it in times of self-doubt just to remind myself that I do indeed belong where I am. I have also learned to give myself a little grace and appreciate the journey.

Indira Hector

Global HR Leader, AstraZeneca

"I think everybody has Imposter Syndrome. You go into an organization like mine where you have a lot of PhDs and MDs. You're sitting at the table, and you want to feel as if you're equally qualified. I have had Imposter Syndrome in my career. Fortunately, I've been sitting at the table for long enough to know that I also bring a lot of value. I have a lot of knowledge in areas that they may not."

If you also suffer from impostor syndrome, you'll have to summon the courage to go outside your comfort zone and socialize with different employees; particularly those who are senior to you. If not, you are setting yourself up to fail. As I mentioned earlier, I encourage you to try new social activities that involve and excite your colleagues as a way to immerse yourself in their world.

That is the exact reason why I learned the fundamentals of golf. I did not want to be left off golf outing lists, as it is still the premier opportunity to network with key executives in most companies. Ninety percent of corporate executives play golf, while 80% say they use it to establish new business relationships![4] To be honest, I do not play well.

But I've at least learned the etiquette and rules of the game. When I'm invited, I do not become a distraction or the center of attention. I can hit the ball straight. I do not take myself too seriously or become angry if I miss a shot. I also know where to stand on the green to avoid messing up someone's line or shot. Learn from me. Do not wait until you are invited to a golf outing to learn how to play. Buy some used clubs and take some lessons to simply learn the ropes. It could have an impact on your career. In fact, if you share with your executives that you are learning golf, they may think of you the next time there is an outing. This is the kind of strategic networking people of color can pursue as they advance within a company.

LESSON 8.3: LEARN WHEN TO CALL ON YOUR ALLIES

Once you've established that networking and being cordial will not automatically cause you to be closer to your peers, the next step is to call on your allies. When cliques form, it's usually due to a powerful central figure who places currency on closeness to him or her. Consequently, workers seek to be in favor with that leader. In a sense, every day at work they are auditioning for a spot higher up in the leader's hierarchy. If this leader is a narcissist, this can become a psychological game, where your peers become more focused on currying favor than doing their job. This can lead to toxic and unhealthy work relationships. Their continual display of fondness for the leader can be draining for the insiders. It's a phony charade they are forced to play to keep their job and try to advance.

Ego-driven leaders will use this in-crowd to centralize their power. It's a simple process of dividing and conquering. If that division is at your expense, do not blame yourself. You are a victim. Once again, a corporate environment should be inclusive. If you're in this situation, the next step is to select whoever you are closest to in the in-crowd. Have a candid conversation with them. Let them know that you feel you are on the outside looking in and that it's hard for you to act with agency to rectify the situation. Ask this person to be your confidant so they can subtly advocate on your behalf. At the end of the day, the primary goal is the overall success of the company.

The Harvard Business Review describes allyship as "a strategic mechanism used by individuals to become collaborators, accomplices, and coconspirators who fight injustice and promote equity in the workplace through supportive personal relationships and public acts of sponsorship and advocacy."[5]

An ally can help you in those tough situations when you're not sure if your boss is biased or just an asshole. They can also strategize with you on how to solve problems of unseen discrimination that may occur. An ally can also provide sage advice. Trusted allies can let you know if you are barking up the wrong tree, or if any of your claims have merit. I cannot overstate how important allies are to a company and to your own personal success. With a proper partnership, you can work together with your ally to improve the environment for all employees. They can also become a constant force in opening lines of communication between the inside group and yourself. In short, an ally can fight for you! It is extremely difficult to be a successful person of color in a corporate environment without allies who have your back. Over time, the hope is that any bias or excluding behaviors start to change. I've personally seen this happen. My allies always looked out for me. Allies can become your eyes and ears in the conference rooms and Zoom rooms from which you have been excluded.

In this way, you can avoid going to human resources to file an official complaint and raise a red flag of discrimination. This is important. Once you cross that line, there is no turning back. In corporate America, we do not believe the victims when it comes to discrimination. Only 1% of employees who file federal discrimination suits win in court.[6] The burden of truth falls on the victim to prove that they were discriminated against with clear-cut evidence free of ambiguity. I've seen this happen all too often.

Indira Hector

Global HR Leader, AstraZeneca

"It's very difficult to prove race discrimination because maybe the manager just doesn't like you. Maybe you just have a really nasty manager and unless it's something very explicit and documented or witnessed by others, it's very, very difficult to prove discrimination based on race. It's very rare. In my career, I've never seen it substantiated."

If there is any shade of gray to the situation, your complaint will be filed away and little or nothing will happen.

Thus, the compelling question here is: Why jeopardize your standing in the company to make a claim so unlikely to go anywhere? You'll most likely suffer more repercussions than the discriminators will. Your work performance and competency may also be met with extra scrutiny. This is a form of retaliation, and it is a terrible place to be because you end up fighting from a position of weakness. Stealthily building internal allies is the way to go if you would like to remain at the company and continue to advance.

LESSON 8.4: WITHOUT DOCUMENTATION, YOU'RE DEFENSELESS

If your efforts don't change the corporate culture and you wish to pursue a claim of discrimination, you must begin the phase of *very meticulous documentation*. You will be asked for specifics, including dates and times that instances of discrimination or exclusion occurred. You should track such examples for at least 90 days and make sure you document your concerns about this issue to your boss as well as human resources.

By this stage, you should start thinking about an exit strategy. You may not have a choice. A company may decide it is easier to give you an exit package than to deal with your situation head-on. You should be prepared for any and all scenarios. Depending on your company and situation, the situation could explode into retaliation. For example, there could be a hypercritical performance review that nudges you out of the company. It is very hard to prove retaliation without meticulous notes. That is why an exit strategy is important to have in your back pocket.

It's imperative in dealing with these situations to always remain calm. It's impossible to ask yourself to be unemotional about such a sensitive topic. By all means, let your frustrations out. You should fully express your feelings in private with a therapist, an executive coach, or a loved one. In work, however, any perception that you are overly emotional can lead to the conclusion that you are immature, unhinged, and unable to perform your job duties. It plays into their hands if they want to retaliate. Companies certainly draw a line in the sand in this way. If you are emotional, they can use this as ammunition to either terminate you or significantly shrink your standing in the company.

Last, but not least, if all else fails, look for a new job. Sometimes, when you've done all you can, it just makes sense to cut your losses and move on. This will be discussed in further detail in Chapter 12: "Learning How to Leave Without Burning Bridges."

I remember coaching a Hispanic employee named Nadia who considered leaving her position due to a very toxic relationship with her boss. She had trouble with the concept of "giving up," as she was raised to stand up and fight for her rights. I remember vividly her saying, "Why should I let them win?" I then told her, "If their 'losing' means you stay in this toxic professional vice grip one day longer, then how are you actually winning?" After a long pause, she agreed. She's now a marketing director at an even bigger firm, earning more money. The last time we spoke, she told me she loved her job and her role has grown immensely over the past two years. Leaving was the best decision she ever made. I was glad I coached her through it.

Robert Childs

Executive Vice President of Enterprise, Inclusion, Diversity, and Business Engagement at American Express

"Take your ball and leave. There are times where you have done everything and it still does not make difference. Embrace the reality that the place you are trying to advance your game, is not the right place for you. Not every work culture is aligned to your values. At some point you will get diminishing returns to your mental health."

CHAPTER 9

Navigate and Survive Bad Bosses

How to Handle Hostile or Biased Bosses in the Workplace

A bad boss is like a disease of the soul.
—*Chetan Bhagat, Author, Columnist, listed as one of Time*
Magazine's 100 most influential people in 2010

Iwas once working as an entry-level analyst at a large health insurance company. One day my supervisor came over to my desk, saying
he wanted to ask me a nagging question. He sat on my desk at my
small cubicle.

> **Timothy S. Taylor**
>
> *Former Senior Counsel of the*
> *New York State United*
> *Teachers Union*
>
> "Keep your eye on the prize.
> Move onto higher ground and
> ignore the petty tyranny of
> small minds. You can call me
> anything you want as long as
> you spell my name correctly
> on your paycheck."

"Errol, you love chicken,
obviously." I blinked. "I was wondering if you have any suggestions
on the best place to get chicken
wings. . . ." He went on to describe
the type of chicken wings he liked.
That they were crunchy on the
outside, soft on the inside, and
not just the small tiny ones, but
larger ones too. I assume he
thought I would know the *really*
good restaurants located in the
outer boroughs, like The Bronx or Queens or areas he'd never both-
ered to explore himself.

All I could think was, *Why is my supervisor asking me about chicken*
wings? I wanted to ignore him—and even tell him how ridiculously
absurd he was being, not to mention racially stereotypical. But instead,
I relented and suggested the first restaurant in Manhattan that
came to mind.

This absurd chicken wings conversation is precisely the type of
bias you will most likely experience in the workplace. For the most
part, the employees you work with are probably not inherently racist,
but they can definitely say and do racist things. Your colleagues will not
wear white hoods and gowns to let you know the hate or bias they
carry in their hearts. The racism you'll most likely will experience will
be subtle and hard to define. Even though racial discrimination in the
workplace was banned under Title VII of the Civil Rights Act of 1964,

it now flies under the radar. It's also not easy to call it out even when you see it. And it surely takes wisdom and emotional intelligence to know when and how to respond. Implicit bias and open hostility are two of the ways you might experience it.

Implicit Bias

One way subtle racism works is when you're overlooked for promotions. This happens when everyone around you is being promoted but your title and salary have stagnated—despite a growing workload. And it is so hard to prove that the reason is due to race. If you bring this up with your HR department, be aware that your leadership team will now have documented evidence that will support, in their view, *why you are not ready for a promotion*. Only raise these types of issues with human resources after you bring it up with your management team. Speaking to your boss first is not as accusatory as going directly to HR. Let your boss know how you feel, but ask in an inquisitive or curious way as opposed to an accusatory manner.

For example, you could say something like: "Molly was promoted, and she has three years of work experience in this space. John was promoted as well, even though he'd never worked in this area of the company. I've been here five years, and I've received only the normal annual pay raise. I'm interested in growing within the company. Can you help me?"

Pauline Bent

Former Vice President at Goldman Sachs, J.P. Morgan, and Pershing

"When I first started out at Goldman Sachs, I found that the men would get the better assignments, higher pay, and easier promotions. When I complained, they would say things like, "Well, don't you want to get married and have kids?" I tried to challenge my managers about moving up because I knew my work was outstanding. One manager was particularly condescending and said, "If you want to get promoted here, you're going to need a college degree." Of course, I already had a college degree! Eventually, I obtained two master's degrees, and started to get recognized. What was frustrating was as a Black female I overperformed—and was expected to overperform!"

By posing the question this way, you avoid coloring the accusation as intentional or, indeed, criminal—even if it is. That's because this could send the management team into a defensive posture. Instead, I give people the benefit of the doubt, and realize that these circumstances may be due to *Implicit Bias*. Often, there can be a corporate fear of promoting or hiring someone who doesn't match the prototype of the usual candidate for a senior position. The hiring manager feels they're going out on a limb to do so. They have a lot to lose and may incur social and professional penalties if their selection of a person of color is flawed in any way. To avoid the potential embarrassment of hiring that person, they instead hire someone who is safer. That is, they decide to take the conventional and more comfortable route. Rather than taking a chance on a high-potential employee of color who never performed the role before, it may feel safer to select a White employee with whom the hiring manager already has a rapport and shared commonalities. That is exactly why companies need diverse leadership teams.

Open Hostility

Another way you can experience racism in the workplace is by facing open hostility or hypercriticism. Unfortunately, I have heard from numerous friends, mentees, and colleagues who have told me about offensive comments that were addressed to them at work. One male associate was frequently called "a puppy dog" by his supervisor because of how nice and friendly he was to work with. Another friend was often greeted with "Hey girl!" by her superior. It made her uncomfortable because it was said in a way to mimic African American Vernacular English, yet her supervisor wasn't Black. It got even worse because her teammates would regularly ask to touch her hair whenever she changed her hairstyle.

You deserve to be respected at work. You have the right to avoid work in a hostile environment. It is important to address these issues in the best way possible to solve the problem at hand rather than creating bigger problems. Next are three rules of the road.

LESSON 9.1: FOLLOW THE "THREE STRIKES" RULE

Give your colleagues the benefit of the doubt. Assume that the comment you found racist or biased was not intended to be so. My rule of thumb is that the first comment is a pass and I will not even respond to it. By the second comment, my awareness of a potential problem is heightened, and I will listen with a critical ear moving forward. I analyze not just what is said to me, but what is communicated to others. I still do not speak to the offender directly, but I may now start to take notes about the incident. Where did it happen? When did it happen? What was the context? And what was my exact response? A good tip for tracking these notes is emailing them to yourself so there is a record. Your company will automatically keep these records as well since they save all of your emails as a matter of business practice. Upon the third incident with someone, it is now time to act. You have observed the behavior three times, and it has been documented at least once.

Documentation is key. If a tree falls in a forest and no one is there to hear it, it did not happen in the corporate world.

LESSON 9.2: PREPARE FOR COURAGEOUS CONVERSATIONS

When you experience the third strike, it's essential to take four major actions.

1. **Do not respond in the moment.** It is likely that your response will be emotional, and your message may not be conveyed. The immediate response will most likely be one of denial or ignorance. This, of course, could potentially upset you even more. **Make sure to bring up your concerns at another time, not in the moment.**

2. **Thoughtfully confront.** When you confront the person about their actions, you may want to add it as the last item to be discussed in an already planned meeting or upcoming

agenda. For example, if you have a future one-on-one meeting with them, bring it up at the end of the meeting as if you were simply trying to be helpful. Here's an example approach:

Since we have a few moments before our call ends, do you mind if I bring up another topic I'd like to discuss? . . . Great. I appreciate that we work well together. And I do appreciate the environment you've created where I can bring up other issues and that you're open to hearing them. So I'd like to tell you that, the other day, last Thursday after the strategic Zoom call we had, you mentioned that you wanted to touch my hair once we returned to the office because you liked the style. I just wanted you to know comments like that don't sit well with me. They make me feel awkward. I'd prefer it if you didn't make such comments. I was going to keep this to myself, but this is the third time I've heard you say something that did not sit right with me. Sorry to unload like this and put you on the spot. But I'm thankful I could express myself.

Please analyze how this was phrased. You are not being accusatory. You are appreciative that they are listening to you. You are describing how their words made you feel. And you are not asking them to validate your feelings. They do not need to agree, because you are sharing your perception. In most instances, the reaction will be an apology or words of embarrassment. Usually, they will be grateful that you brought it to their attention and that you are also not criticizing them.

3. **Keep leaders in the loop:** The next step is to tell your boss that you had this conversation with your colleague. If it is your boss who made these comments, then it is important to bring this to the attention of your boss's supervisor. This can create angst for all the parties involved. To keep these conversations as constructive and productive as possible, send a simple note to your boss's supervisor requesting that they meet with you for 10–15 minutes regarding a personal matter. You may or may not get a response, but at least you

will have it documented that you attempted to resolve the issue internally. That is a very important step along this arduous process.

4. **Don't leave out HR:** Tell someone in Human Resources that you had this discussion. Many companies assign an HR business partner to each division or department. You should know who they are and reach out. This is a part of your documentation process that needs to take place. Just let them know about your meeting and exactly what transpired. There should also be an email that you send to yourself to document that you brought this up with HR. You can also send a confirmation email to HR to confirm that you both communicated.

From there, you wait. Best-case scenario: This behavior never happens again. And nothing needs to happen beyond these actions. Worst-case scenario: The offensive or racist behavior continues. Now, you only deal with HR and keep your boss abreast of your actions. Since you already spoke with them directly, the hard part is done. Once again, it is wise to give them the benefit of the doubt.

LESSON 9.3: HANDLING A BIASED OR RACIST BOSS

Early in my career I remember heading out to a Thai lunch with one of my bosses and several members of my team. As we descended in the elevator at our corporate headquarters, the topic of difficult projects came up. We were all describing our worst projects when the conversation finally came around to me. I detailed the highly stressful time when I was the lead product analyst of a large initiative impacting our organization. We were doing a data-matching analysis called a disruption report, and I'd finished the analysis in the eleventh hour. As we walked through the hustle and bustle of the New York City streets, I shared with my team how worried I'd been about missing the deadline. It had taken longer than expected because I had had to combine four different databases that I had built from scratch.

Sachin H. Jain, MD, MBA

Recognized by Modern Healthcare magazine *as one of American healthcare's 100 most influential leaders*

"Actually, one of my most challenging situations was with an Indian American boss who felt super threatened by the fact that I was also a successful Indian American executive. We were both separately nominated for an award. My boss actually had his Chief of Staff call me to say, "Your boss would really like you to withdraw from this because it reflects badly if there's two people from the same organization who are nominated for this award." I couldn't believe it, and at the end of the day I stayed in—knowing my days would be short in the culture. The Indian American boss really created a very difficult situation for me. A year later, he reached out: "It looks like we haven't done a good job of keeping in touch or saying nice things about each other. I'd like to stay in better touch." I left the text message unanswered. No way. No interest."

That is when my boss chimed in, "Good thing for you, Errol. If you didn't get that analysis done, they would have hanged you!" The team joined him in a chuckle. But for me, time slowed down . . .

Did he just say they would have hanged me?

I paused in those interminable moments, but did not respond. It was quiet. An uneasy pregnant silence.

I eventually responded, "Yes, I'm glad I got it done."

The conversation meandered into different topics, but I was in a totally different world. Indeed, I felt like I was on Mars. Insensitive remarks can stop you in your tracks. And that's exactly what happened. I immediately became silent and withdrawn.

One of the worst things to endure is having a horrible boss. I've been there. I once had a boss who took credit for all my work and used information as currency within the organization. He purposely kept me oblivious to important news and developments that would allow me to do my job better. Once I realized these behaviors were not going to change, I left internally—making a lateral move within the company to a different department. In fact, this is very typical of corporate America. A 2022 study entitled "Horrible Bosses: Are American Workers Quitting Their Jobs or Quitting Their Managers?" found that 82% of American workers would quit their job due to a bad manager.[1]

It's been said that people do not quit jobs; they quit their bosses. That's why it's so important to realize that at your next interview you're not just interviewing for a new job—you're also interviewing for a new boss. Title and salary are key components of a new role, but selecting the right boss is paramount to both. During an interview process, ask the tough questions to get a level of comfort with your potential new leader. What is their stance on DE&I programs? What successes have they had in increasing opportunities for underrepresented employee populations? Do they have tangible examples of coaching and mentoring employees of color successfully? The best way to avoid a bad boss is to not have one in the first place. But if you are not so fortunate, the following are three options to take when you have a nasty boss.

1. **Leave internally.** Find a new role within your organization under a new leader or department head. You can even have a "Come to Jesus" meeting with your boss to basically express "I see the writing on the wall. If you help me find a new position, I'll fill my role with someone with whom you are more aligned." Calling out the elephant in the room can be scary, but it has its advantages. Why is this important? Because if you get a poor performance rating, you will find it difficult to move into a new position internally. Any hiring manager within your company who has half a brain will want to see your prior performance reviews, particularly your most recent one. Thus, it is imperative to negotiate with your boss about your exit plan so you can ensure a favorable review upon leaving.

   This is where your professional network is vital. You should have relationships *before* you start looking for a new job internally. The worst situation to be in is one where you are forced to introduce yourself and bond with new people *while* you are trying to find a new gig. Believe it or not, your desperation comes through. And you never want to appear desperate in this game.

I recently helped Kevin, a Black male employee at another company, who suddenly needed to find a new job because his department was shutting down. The project he was working on was coming to an end. The team overall was not meeting their revenue targets, so after three years of underperformance, the project would come to end within six months. He had not networked with the vice president or other senior leaders within the company prior to the closing announcement. I coached him on how to introduce himself to those executives who could potentially hire him before his job ended. It was not easy for him to establish these new relationships while having a ticking clock. In the end, I helped him, and he was able to successfully find a new role in the company. But not everyone will have such success. It's important to build bridges before you have to cross them.

2. **Leave externally.** Job-hopping used to be frowned upon by employers. A long tenure at a company denoted ethics, reliability, and loyalty. When employers saw a resume with many companies and positions on it, it was looked at suspiciously. However, it is now a reality that workers from younger generations like Gen Z (Zoomers) and Gen Y (Millennials) are the least likely to hold a long-term job. In fact, a Department of Labor study in 2019 noted that Baby Boomers held an average of more than 12 jobs between ages 18 and 52, with 75% of these positions lasting less than five years.[2] That means that employers are getting more accustomed to seeing people come and go, with their resumes containing multiple pit stops along the way.

All of this has a direct influence on your success and advancement. Be conscious of how often you move and be able to articulate *why* you moved. What opportunities did the new position bring you? How did your role grow in scope? If you moved laterally, be clear about the reasons behind your move. In the past, I've told recruiters and hiring managers that I was moving laterally to have a higher ceiling for growth. That is, there were limited career advancement opportunities at my previous position and moving laterally to a new company with more opportunities made the most sense. In this manner, I conveyed that I had a plan for my career. That I was intentional in moving laterally. Most importantly, I was not *running away* from a role, but *running to a new* one.

3. **Just leave.** Yes, it's much harder to find a job when you're unemployed. But let's say you can't find another job that's at least a lateral move, whether internally or externally. You've been at your job a year or so. Your boss is still nasty, and you're constantly bringing your work issues home. For the sake of your own health and wellness, you should think about leaving. Or if, worse yet, you're drowning in anxiety and/or depression, leaving may be the best option.

Sadly, I've worked with colleagues who have stayed too long toiling for a terrible boss.

Sachin H. Jain, MD, MBA

Recognized by Modern Healthcare magazine *as one of American healthcare's 100 most influential leaders in healthcare*

"The truth is that a lot of people will tell you to hang in there and wait it out. I would say culture is culture. I would really encourage people to move on when they're part of a racist culture. The biggest mistakes I've made in my career were staying when I was the subject to abuse, whether racially motivated or not. People suddenly feel all this loyalty. They have loyalty to their team, loyalty to their peers, to the customers or the patients. I think that is very misplaced. When you are being abused, the worst thing you can do is just to keep taking it. Success is the best form of revenge."

I watched them actually change as human beings. One colleague, Mary, was fixated on her relationship with her toxic boss. It consumed her life to the extent that even all her personal conversations were about work. I found that I distanced myself from her because speaking with her literally changed my own demeanor. Her depression and frustration rubbed off on me. She began to lose her self-esteem, believing she deserved the treatment she was getting. But abuse is abuse, whether it's physical, emotional, or psychological. **Don't tolerate abuse!**

So, if you need to, you should quit a toxic job. However, you'll also need to put a game plan in place before you exit. I recommend waiting until you have at least three job opportunities in full swing with the strong possibility that one of them will land. Also, personal savings is key. Your depression will not subside if you add worrying about paying bills to your list. Saving at least six months of your pay-check in a special bank account prior to your resignation will allow you to focus on a new role without the strain of financial pressure. You need to avoid making a fast decision on a position out of financial necessity, which may not ultimately be the best decision for your future and career.

One other thing, if your human resources team conducts an exit interview: *Be honest!* Tell the unvarnished truth about your experiences. There is nothing like the departure of a very talented person to shake up the leadership team and let them know there is a problem. The best gift you can give an organization upon your exit is to tell them the truth. Many folks who have resigned treated their exit interview as perfunctory and did not delve into details. I have personally called for-mer colleagues or team members who have resigned to find out what led to their decision. They usually open up and share all the juicy gos-sip on their horrible experiences, but by then, it is too late. That's the real shame. If there is opportunity and time, I always try to tell them "give me the last right of refusal." I ask them to warn me before they leave. This way, I can try to be a champion on their behalf and possibly mediate the situation they are facing. This is also essential advice for all: before leaving, you should ensure that you have exhausted all of your resources. Often, abused employees don't give themselves the time to properly calculate the cost or learning curve of joining a new company. Sometimes, fighting to stay is better. Especially if you have an ally, mentor, or champion in your corner.

Pauline Bent

Former Vice President at Goldman Sachs, J.P. Morgan, and Pershing

"When I was a hiring manager, I made sure to bring in minorities. That was how I felt I was trying to change the organization. I participated in the recruitment for undergraduate schools. I went to all the graduate schools and made sure to have minorities come on board. You know, you have to kind of change it from the inside. That was my main regret for resigning. That would have been the better way in retrospect. To continue to bring as many minorities in to change the company internally, because once I was out, there's nothing I could do. I felt like I gave up my power. But you don't realize that until you're in such a situation. I think it's better if you fight within the organization and make changes that way."

CHAPTER 10

Grow by Giving Back

Experience the Power of Public Service and Selflessness

Service to others is the rent you pay for your room here on Earth.
—*Muhammad Ali, legendary American boxer and activist*

Lessons of leadership can be learned from a worldwide variety of sources, including public service. If there is one thing I learned, it is this: just because someone has the title of boss does not mean they are a leader.

A famous fellow Fordham University alum, Donald McGannon, once said appropriately, "Leadership is action, not a position."[1] And rightly so. Donald McGannon was one of the most influential broadcasting executives in America during the 1960s and 1970s. He became the President and Chairman of the Westinghouse Broadcasting Company (WBC) at the ripe old age of 35.[2]

At the time, Westinghouse was made up of four television and five radio stations, which made it the largest independent TV–radio ownership operation in the entire country. McGannon owed much of his success to having a strong mentor, Chris J. Witting, who convinced him to leave the oil and coal industry and join Witting in the media industry at the DuMont Television Network in 1951. When Mr. Witting was promoted to Vice President of the Westinghouse Electric Corporation, the parent company of WBC, he made sure McGannon assumed his former position that had been left vacant.[3] This is merely one of thousands of stories that punctuate the importance of mentors and champions.

McGannon strongly believed that "Radio and television were both powerful media, although in separate ways. To him, radio was in a period of rebirth after the impact of television. Its new role in the millions of American houses today is unique and cannot be filled by any other medium. It is no less dynamic but now operates in a different atmosphere."[4] McGannon made these prophetic statements about radio in 1956, just after the television invaded American households. One could easily surmise that McGannon envisioned an industry like today, where so much content is delivered through podcasts, which lack the visual stimulation of television but are now ever so relevant in our media landscape.

Donald McGannon also did not take this power and influence for granted. He dedicated his life to using his position of authority for the welfare of all. McGannon led the charge to ban televised cigarette ads during a time when it was a very unpopular stance. He also leveraged his firm's political capital to tighten broadcasting standards and regulations to further protect the public. He was also a prominent supporter of using television programming to properly educate America.[5]

Originally born in the South Bronx, McGannon also stood out as an advocate of social responsibility in broadcasting too: using television for the good of the world.[6] If he were alive today, I can only assume he would strongly advocate banning propagandist "news" networks. I also think he would call for social media tech giants to hold themselves more accountable for the misinformation that is passed on to the public through their platforms.

Most importantly, McGannon not only held deeply rooted beliefs in racial and gender equity, but also had the courage to lead with action. On October 30, 1968, the *New York Times* broke the news that George Norford, the first African American producer of network television programs, had been hired by McGannon as Vice President and General Executive of the Westinghouse Broadcasting Company.[7] This made Mr. Norford the highest ranking African American in the entire broadcasting industry.

McGannon pushed for racial equality in a variety of other ways as well. He became the President of the National Urban League (NUL) in the 1970s while the famed Vernon Jordan was serving as the Executive Director. The National Urban League was founded in 1910 and, at the time, was one of the most prominent and leading nonpartisan national civil rights organizations. Based in New York City, the NUL fought for economic and social justice for African Americans while taking a very public stance against all forms of racial discrimination in the United States. For a White man to be the president of such an organization during the 1970s is a testament to the character of Donald McGannon. His influence as a change agent and a leader in both broadcasting and civil rights would lead the NUL to eventually create an annual award in his name, the highest distinction given by them.[8] Clearly, McGannon made leadership an action in his time on Earth and used public service as an important vehicle in doing so.

Giving back to your community is an amazing way to learn various leadership lessons, which is key to your personal growth and professional development. I cannot underscore enough the importance of volunteerism in your path to the top. The compassion and empathy of McGannon opened further doors of opportunity for himself and others. Yes, many of us feel that our time is limited and our schedules are way too tight. We use this as an excuse to bypass opportunities to serve others. Trust me, however, that these are the very experiences that turn into *Willy Wonka*–type "golden tickets" in corporate America. You may have years of expertise at a company, but you may lack a true variety of experiences, and thus have a limited vantage point. In a competitive environment like corporate America, that can be the difference between grabbing a key position or being the *second-best* contender. Experience trumps longevity.

I have counseled employees who have been in the same role for years and wondered why they have not advanced. I always explain that if you design your role over the years to be irreplaceable, then you will not be replaced. You will be layered. How do employees do this? By building efficiencies and being open to new opportunities. Always try to broaden your experiences. One of the ways to do this is through public service. Mahatma Gandhi also famously said, "The best way to find yourself is to lose yourself in the service of others."

I certainly lost myself in service to young Black and Brown boys from The Bronx, starting in 2008 while I was wearing a tuxedo and sitting at a gala in the middle of Manhattan. At the time, the CEO of my company had sponsored a table at the annual gala of an organization called 100 Black Men. As I dined on a steak dinner with fine wine galore, the evening progressed to the award ceremonies.

An energetic brother with magnetic charisma stepped up on stage and addressed the large crowd from the podium. His name was David C. Banks. He enthusiastically described his brand-new, all-boys public school, Eagle Academy, situated just a stone's throw from Yankee Stadium in the same impoverished section of The Bronx where Don McGannon had grown up. Banks had grandiose plans of expanding all over New York City precisely in the hot spots of the prison pipeline.

His words were enthralling, emphatic, and magical. I was fully captivated and remember his words to this day.

"We are looking for a few good brothers to get off the sidelines and get into the game and come mentor." These words resonated with me so much. At the time, I was a business consultant at a for-profit health insurance company, and the opportunity to give back to my Bronx community was irresistible. I was longing to give back to my zip code. The Black community has seen a plethora of motivational speakers, but Mr. Banks was different. He was dynamic, inspiring, and one hell of a change maker.

I signed up that night and began mentoring at his school less than a month later. The most amazing thing when I first entered the school building one Saturday morning was seeing Mr. Banks there in the flesh elevating his students as they gathered in the cafeteria. As the assembly started, they began to chant loudly a poem called *Invictus*.

Imagine close to 300 Black and Brown boys in gray-blue uniforms yelling

> *Out of the night that covers me,*
> *Black as the Pit from pole to pole,*
> *I thank whatever gods may be*
> *For my unconquerable soul.*
>
> *In the fell clutch of circumstance*
> *I have not winced nor cried aloud.*
> *Under the bludgeonings of chance*
> *My head is bloody, but unbowed.*
>
> *Beyond this place of wrath and tears*
> *Looms but the Horror of the shade,*
> *And yet the menace of the years*
> *Finds, and shall find, me unafraid.*
>
> *It matters not how strait the gate,*
> *How charged with punishments the scroll,*
> *I am the master of my fate:*
> *I am the captain of my soul.*

Their chants gave me goose bumps. This man and his school were changing the lives of so many. The education happening within these four walls was special. *But why were these young men chanting the words of this 19th centruy Latin poem? Invictus* is Latin for the inability to be conquered or being undefeated.[9] When William Earnest Henley wrote this poem in 1875, he already had an amputated leg. He sat in his hospital bed describing the pain and agony of fighting for his life in the face of death as he proceeded with risky surgery to save his other leg.[10] The poem vividly speaks to holding on to your pride and your self-worth through whatever calamities the world throws your way.

In the same way, these Black and Brown boys have to contend with so many obstacles in their lives. Society was against them in every which way. Police officers target them, and the prospects of their success are slim as the statistics are not in their favor. Simply surviving is a victory. Yet, every single day, they put on their school uniforms, walk through the concrete jungles of The Bronx, get together with their fellow classmates, and shout that they are the masters of their own fate. The lack of New York State funding, the crime on their block, or New York City's poor infrastructure or dilapidated housing projects. . . . None of these factors determined the outcome of their lives. These students decided that nothing would stop them.

My first day volunteering at their school was nothing short of life transforming. I dived into mentoring after going through formal mentor training. I was paired with several students and began a journey of helping teenage kids navigate through life and pursue their dreams.

I formed a very close relationship to one student in particular, Ja'Paris. We connected well and began to speak about life. When we met, Ja'Paris told me he did not really care about his future. He confessed that he could not see a world in which he would be an older adult functioning in society. School was not a priority for him. He did not have an easy upbringing and hung out with the wrong crowd. He was so estranged from his father that he regretted sharing his last name. That comment really stuck with me. As a single Black man at the time, I longed for the day of bringing children into this world, creating a legacy, and passing on my father Stuart's good name.

As our relationship developed, Ja'Paris' anger toward the world slowly subsided. He began thinking about his future years in high school, and indeed, a life after graduation. The first key for Ja'Paris was to actually *see* his future. Then, we could work together and begin to *mold* it. I remember giving him my business card and telling him that if he ever needed anything, he had all my contact information right there, including my cell phone number. The school year soon came to an end, and Ja'Paris and I would part ways during the summer months until the following fall.

One summer day at work, I missed a call, which went straight to voicemail. I was not able to hear the message until later in the day due to back-to-back meetings. I finally listened and could not believe my ears. An NYPD Sergeant had left me a message demanding that I call him back immediately. I had to listen to the message a few times to calm myself. It finally hit me. The Sergeant who had left me a message was Juan Santiago, a recent Fordham graduate and classmate whom I ran track with. I was confused. *How did he get my phone number? Who was he calling about?*

I quickly called him back. It was great to hear his familiar voice. After brief pleasantries, Sergeant Santiago explained that he had picked up my mentee, Ja'Paris, after a brawl between high school students. He was with several other teenagers involved in the fight. After arresting the students and bringing them back to the precinct, Ja'Paris had been searched. Sergeant Santiago had gone through his wallet and stumbled upon my business card. Santiago was stunned to see my name and asked Ja'Paris about it. Ja'Paris had explained that "Mr. Errol" was his mentor in a high school program on Saturday mornings. Santiago told Ja'Paris he would call me to verify the information.

I couldn't believe it. "Yes, I know Ja'Paris! I'm his mentor!" I asked if he'd been arrested. Santiago explained the situation and assured me it would end well. Santiago later questioned Ja'Paris about why he was hanging out with the wrong crowd. Ja'Paris would soon show up to court to face his charges and found that none of his arrest-ing officers showed up. *Case dismissed!*

If it hadn't been for my business card, this whole group of teens fighting in the streets would have ended up with a record. I tried to steady myself as I thought about the power of volunteering. The power of giving back to your community. I also thought about redemption. I once was locked up as an undergrad student many moons ago without anyone to call for help. My being able to help Ja'Paris in this way was full circle. It made me realize that I was right where I was supposed to be . . . giving back to the people of The Bronx.

Ja'Paris would eventually turn his life around through more mentoring sessions. He changed his outlook on life, improved his grades, built stronger relationships with his fellow students and teachers, and started thinking optimistically about his future. One of my highest honors was driving Ja'Paris to college after he graduated high school and helping him move into his dorm (Figure 10.1). I could not have been prouder in that moment.

Volunteering changed my life as much as it changed that of Ja'Paris. I wanted to do even more for Eagle Academy and ran for an open board seat of 100 Black Men, the nonprofit organization. I won and became one of its youngest board members. I was able to hone my

Figure 10.1   Move-in day with Ja'Paris, August 15, 2015.

leadership skills even more by learning about governance, finance, program development, management, and fund raising.

Through this new board role, I was also able to not only be a mentor to young men but also a mentee to some of the most influential Black executives in New York City with whom I shared a board seat—all thanks to a speech from David C. Banks many years prior. Mr. Banks taught me inspirational leadership, the importance of follow-through, and how execution breeds credibility and the confidence of others. Eagle Academy now has six schools in New York City and New Jersey, and a foundation that educates and empowers schools serving young men of color across the country. One of my favorite events to attend at Eagle Academy is the Tie Ceremony, where mentors come and help the students tie their new tie around their neck because of their new grade. Figure 10.2 is from a Tie Ceremony in 2016 at the Eagle Academy of Harlem. As one of the first hires by

Figure 10.2   Errol Pierre with David Banks, October 14, 2016.

recently elected New York City Mayor Eric Adams, David C. Banks is now the Public Schools Chancellor of the largest school district in the country![11]

LESSON 10.1: SOMETIMES THE BEST WAY TO BE SELFISH IS TO BE SELFLESS

Nonprofit volunteering is a great way to give back to the community and align yourself with a cause that speaks to your heart. There are so many ways to volunteer. I started volunteering for the West Side YMCA, located across the street from Central Park, back in 2008 as a member of their Program Development Committee. I was able to solve problems with the leadership team of the YMCA and help bring them resources and other tools to be successful. I became a board member in 2010 at 27 years of age. As a board member, I was confronted with payroll issues, staffing shortages, building maintenance concerns, fundraising needs, and overall strategic planning.

Despite not having much managerial experience under my belt at work, I gained real-life organizational and administrative experience as a volunteer board member. *The skills I learned as a board member were 100% transferrable to the corporate setting.* I do believe my experiences with the YMCA accelerated my growth at my day job. Volunteering was the goal, but advancement became the by-product. Helping people is the greatest gift of all. But you'll learn some things along the way too.

LESSON 10.2: LEADERSHIP IS THE #1 TRANSFERRABLE SKILL

It's important to have proficiency in your line of work, but it's also easy to get bogged down as a subject-matter expert. In order to keep your options open, you'll want to hone and perfect the your leadership skill set for the rest of your career. An additional plus is the fact that leadership brings out the talents of people exponentially. When you inspire people to be better versions of themselves, offering a clear vision and the feeling of support and empowerment, you set up teams for success.

Don McGannon moved from the oil industry to become the most influential person in television. But his oil and gas expertise weren't enough. It was his leadership, his vision, his charisma, his uncompromising set of values. Those were the attributes that made him successful while he transformed his industry in the process. Lead with leadership and the rest will follow.

Sachin H. Jain, MD, MBA

Recognized by Modern Healthcare magazine *as one of American healthcare's 100 most influential leaders*

"You know leadership is explicitly tied to followership. It's fundamentally about winning the hearts and minds of people to drive positive change. That's what leadership is."

CHAPTER 11

Be Honest Even When It's Hard

Truth Telling Can Set You Apart in the Workplace

Truth stands, even if there be no public support. It is self-sustained.
—Mahatma Gandhi

Yfou likely know about legendary Danish writer Hans Christian Andersen and his 1837 fairy tale, *The Emperor's New Clothes*—but here is a brief refresher. It describes a king who is duped into buying a very expensive outfit that could only be seen by the smartest of men who were fit for their position. The king paid a large sum of money for the clothes to be made. Upon his final exhibition, he refused to admit that he could not see his clothes because that would reveal he was unqualified to be king. All the men around him also lied and claimed they could also see his magnificent clothing. This charade led to a public procession with the king parading these new garments across his kingdom. It took two innocent children to point out that his "costume" was a sham and the king was naked. Everyone in the kingdom finally came clean. By that time, the swindlers had left the city with bags and bags of money.[1]

The moral of the story has a direct application to the corporate world: when a leader surrounds himself with "Yes" men or women, it often leads to embarrassing results. It is far better as a leader to surround yourself with an honest team of people who are unafraid to ask questions or to point out shortcomings as they see them.

I had a personal opportunity to either be a "Yes" man or that little child who declared that the king was naked. My CEO and President once invited me to meet the then-Presidential candidate, Barack Obama, at the Nasdaq headquarters in 2007. I was elated at the invite when it came through my Outlook email. I was going to have this unique opportunity to meet a man who many believed could be the first Black President of the United States. It was humbling to think that my CEO handpicked me out of close to 5,000 employees to be one of the few who would be one of his esteemed guests. I immediately called my parents and told them about the opportunity. My dad was particularly flabbergasted. I also told my small group of close friends. They too were as surprised and encouraged me to get there early and take lots of pictures.

At that time, there was such a fervor for Barack Obama among the Black community. African Americans, Caribbean Americans, and the ever-growing African Diaspora in America all embraced Obama as a force for good. For them, he was a giant symbol of who we could be in this country if we work hard. My parents did not believe that in their lifetime that they would see a Black President in America. Barack Obama now represented that dream.

I recall my mother calling me, shocked and surprised at the news. "Why did he pick you?" "I don't know, Mom!" "What did you do?" She said in an inquisitive and almost accusatory tone. As if to say, *please give me some more context so I can understand what is happening to my child.*

You see, my mother is different than my dad. For her, good news always came with speculation and concern. In her mind, there had to be a reason why I was picked, and she wondered if the decision had ulterior motives. As a recent immigrant to this country, Mom passed through America in a very different manner than I did. Nothing was given to her. She worked hard for every bit of her success. She also came to America leery of people. There is an instant skepticism of immigrants when they arrive in a new country without knowing the language well. My immigrant parents, especially my mother, formed hardened hearts to this new American world and maintained a more distrusting eye. I felt this suspicion like a dark weighted blanket thrown upon me and any of the achievements that I brought home. My spirits deflated when I discussed with my mom why I was chosen to meet the Presidential candidate. After all, it was a great question: *Why did the CEO choose me?*

It did not make much sense, as I was only a business development consultant at the time. I had limited exposure to my CEO, and I was not his direct report. In fact, I was several layers below him in the company hierarchy. We hadn't spoken about politics in the past, nor did he know any of my personal feelings about the candidate. Maybe my mother was on to something with her questioning. Frustrated, I quickly ended the call with her. After I hung up, I decided to leave the question unanswered and focus on way more important things . . . like what I would wear to the event!

The idea of meeting then-candidate Barack Obama gave me butterflies. These are the moments in your life that you can describe to your children and grandchildren! How many people experience exposure to such a historical figure?

I envisioned a closed-door meeting over a large antique wooden conference table with Evian water bottles on marble coasters stationed in front of each seat. I knew there would be other key business leaders from New York in attendance as well. I imagined CEOs of other prominent companies at the table in their dark solid and pinstriped suits. I knew enough to realize that I most likely would not have a seat at the boardroom table. But I figured I would at least be in the room and could take one of the seats in the back. Was my CEO grooming me for a future leadership role? Is that why he wanted me to attend the meeting?

The invite came from my CEO's executive assistant. It stated that I was cordially invited to join my CEO to this meeting at the Nasdaq headquarters in New York. No one else was listed on the email. I could not see who else would be attending.

It was February 2007. At the time, the economy was beginning to falter. Stock prices fell, and Alan Greenspan, then Chair of the Federal Reserve, was publicly predicting a recession. This was also the start of Freddie Mac pulling back from investing in subprime loans, the earliest indication that we were in a volatile housing bubble. By this time, a real estate investment trust specializing in subprime lending, New Century, would file for bankruptcy. American Home Mortgages would follow suit, and by the summer, Bear Stearns would liquidate two of its hedge funds. NetBank would also file for bankruptcy while Countrywide Mortgage was borrowing $11.5 billion from 40 different banks in order to stay open. The American economy was in a free fall.

Candidate Obama was coming to New York and meeting with approximately 150 Wall Street executives at the Nasdaq headquarters to give a speech about how he would reform the financial industry, protect Americans with mortgages, and offer help to middle-class Americans. He was to highlight several financial and tax reforms during his speech, but his message to Wall Street was that more regulations, scrutiny, and oversight were coming their way.

I will never forget that that day, Monday, September 17, 2007. It was impossible to fall asleep the night before. I was so excited about what this grand meeting would be. I tossed and turned the whole night, occasionally staring at the ceiling in the wee hours of the morning.

It was a Monday, so I knew going into the office was going to be hectic, especially because public schools had just reopened. I left extra early and had to take a different subway route, which added to my anxiety. I got off at Times Square where the Nasdaq headquarters were located. Exiting the subway, I remember looking up at all the intimidating skyscrapers surrounding me. As I got closer to the address, I could feel the butterflies in my belly beginning to flutter.

Walking in, I saw scores of reporters lingering around the lobby. As I maneuvered through the crowd, I stumbled upon Jonathan, a fellow employee from my company. *What was he doing here?*

Jonathan didn't work in our corporate office with me. He worked in our Brooklyn office, where our operational teams were located. Mind you, I worked on the executive floor, the same floor as my CEO, in our corporate office in Manhattan. I assumed my close proximity to the CEO was the reason I made the list. But if Jonathan also made this elite list, who else was invited?

We were directed to go to a specific floor where the meeting would be happening. Security asked for our names and company. As they looked for us on the list, I could not help but notice a long guest list attached to my company. I grabbed my nametag and waited for Edwin.

We rode the elevator to the appropriate floor, entered a big hallway, and bumped into a slew of more co-workers from my job. We all recognized each other and began to walk as a group into the main seating area. It was now five of us inching our way forward. As we approached the front, we quickly learned that only invited guests were allowed in the executive front section with seating. Up there, these executive guests could see the podium and the stage from which Obama would be speaking. This executive section was bordered by a barricade that prevented other guests from entering or exiting. Behind that section was a row of seats for the press and media cameras.

Behind the press was where we were, a rear section where guests of the invited guests were allowed to loiter. Where we stood, there were no seats, and our view of the front was obscured by the media. Two more co-workers joined our group, bringing the total number to seven. None of us had had any idea the others were coming, as we each had received the invites separately. As I gazed at our group of standing employees, all here to see candidate Obama, it hit me like a ton of bricks. Everyone invited was Black.

A sea of thoughts and questions ran through my mind. First, what an awesome opportunity to meet a Presidential candidate who could potentially make history. But did our CEO specifically handpick only his Black employees? While maybe it made sense to bring those employees to see Obama, it forced me to realize how low in the organization he had to go to find enough African Americans like me to invite. There weren't enough of us in the middle or higher levels of management to pull a list of 10.

While we were invited and able to be in the room during the speech, it was impossible to see Barack Obama or even our own CEO, who was seated in the front. On top of that, the other 149 New York business leaders looked a lot less like us. Do you get it? Whites in front, Blacks way behind.

When Obama concluded his speech to great applause, he began to walk through the crowd and shake hands. We all tried to squeeze and push to the front, but by the time we got even slightly close, Obama was already heading to the exits. I remember leaving the Nasdaq headquarters on my own. I tried to see if I could locate my CEO and head back with him, but I lost him in the sea of people. I had dressed up for nothing.

On the subway ride back to my downtown office, I wondered why I had been invited in the first place. I was curious if the invitation was to simply show the candidate that my company had diverse employees. Or did my company want to extend this invitation to our Black employees as a token of appreciation? Either way, I felt small and used as a pawn. Of course, I would have preferred to have been invited on my merits rather than my skin color.

I returned to the office and turned on my computer. There it was, sitting in my inbox. An email from the CEO. He asked for feedback on the event and wondered if I enjoyed myself. I had a quick decision to make. Do I provide authentic feedback or just say: "*It was awesome.*

Thanks for the opportunity"? Should I be a "Yes" man or should I tell the emperor he had no clothes? I decided to let the emperor know he was butt naked.

For some strange compelling reason, I wrote back a long-winded reply:

> When I received the invite, I thought I was special. I thought I was handpicked because of my value to the company. I thought the invitation was solely for me. I had worn my best suit, got a haircut, and had excitedly told my parents about this amazing event. However, when I arrived, I realized I was invited with nine other Black colleagues as well. The most depressing aspect of this group was that it included the highest-ranking Black employees we have, including our General Counsel. Even though I was only a consultant at the time, it dawned on me that I made the list as one of the 10 Black employees to attend this prestigious event.
>
> This was not all. We did not get to sit with our CEO who also attended but he was able to watch from an executive section in the front the room. We were forced to watch from the back of the room, way behind the mics and cameras of the media. I assumed I was going to meet candidate Obama. No such luck. He was so far in front of the room with the invited executives that he never made his way to the back. There was too much security for us to try to move forward to meet him. It soon became clear that our company was the only one to bring so many guests. When I realized this, I suddenly felt like a pawn, selected only because of the color of my skin and not because I was a valued employee.

I hit SEND. The damage had been done. This was the feedback I provided to my CEO!

I thought I would be fired or at least demoted. My phone rang. The CEO's executive assistant asked me to come down to his office. That was perhaps my longest walk down any hallway. The walk was the easy part. The hard part was waiting to enter his large and intimidating office: a corner office with its own conference table, giant sofa, and

Timothy S. Taylor

Former Senior Counsel of the New York State United Teachers Union

"When I first started working at law firms, I was the only Black person working there. My expectations were very low for how they were going to treat me. I was never under the illusion that I would be invited to the senior partner's house for Sunday brunch. They may praise you or serve you a steak, but meanwhile are limiting your opportunities or not giving you the plum assignments. They may stop you from meeting those clients or decision makers who can make or break your career. When you scratch beneath the surface, it's simply tribalism or us versus them. People protecting their turf. Racism still persists behind closed doors. The powers that be still put you in boxes but don't tell you."

spectacular views overlooking the New York City skyline. I thought to myself how rarely I had ever been in the CEO's office—let alone by myself.

I was also scared that the CEO's response would be to tell me he didn't have to invite me to the event in the first place. Often, when people of color do complain, a common but coded retort is: *You should be happy with what you get; it could be a lot worse.* This is a silent message expressed through gestures and deeds that we learn as employees of color in corporate America. These statements are never said out loud, but you can definitely feel them.

The CEO called me in. He was as intimidating as his office. A tall White man, he sat down and gazed at me for a moment. Then he began to speak. He shared that this had been something he had been thinking about. I told him how amazing I felt to have been invited but was dismayed to see every other Black employee from our floor there, including our General Counsel. It showed me that our bench was not that deep, particularly if I made the cut as a consultant.

The CEO thanked me for my honesty. He wanted to increase diversity, equity, and inclusion (DE&I) in the company and was strongly committed to it as an executive. He appreciated feedback like this so that the company could do better.

"Can you keep telling me the truth?" he asked.

I smiled and said yes. And I certainly did. From that moment on, our relationship began to grow closer as well. He would email me directly asking for data and information. My confidence grew as I felt more comfortable emailing him back and sharing my true opinion on business matters. He took time out to check in with me and ensure that I felt seen, heard, and supported.

Within a few months, I was promoted to my first managerial role, supervising a team of nine sales associates. I also was quickly recruited to join the company's first diversity and inclusion committee, speaking truth to power without fear of retribution or retaliation.

Then one day, a few years later, the CEO called me into his office and asked me if I would be his Chief of Staff, reporting directly to him. Once again, he appreciated my candor, my insights, and matter-of-factness.

I happily accepted the role and looked forward to the opportunity to work even more closely with my CEO. This role catapulted my career. All because I was crazy enough to send an email telling my truth. It would have been so much easier to lie, but sometimes the easiest decisions are not always the best ones.

Robert Childs

Executive Vice President of Enterprise, Inclusion, Diversity and Business Engagement at American Express

"There are many things I attribute to the success I have had so far:

Be Curious: Understand how things work and how your actions impact others.

Stay Open Minded: Be open to different points of view as your job when you are a leading is to make the best-informed decision you have at that moment.

Be True to Your Words and Actions: Own the results of your actions, learn from them, and get better each time.

Relationships Matter: There is an African proverb that resonated with me: "If you want to go fast, go alone. If you want to go far, go together." I interpreted this to mean in order to sustain yourself and the journey you are on, there will be times you go alone and times you need others, whether they are peers, work for you, are mentors, advocates or sponsors. They all matter."

I was once told by an executive that my *Achilles heel* in business was my conscience. In the moment, the true meaning of the comment did not resonate. But today, if that is my biggest weakness, I wear it as a badge of honor. Honesty does not always make you the most popular person in the room. But you will be respected for your values and your resolve. That level of respect is priceless.

LESSON 11.1: BE BRAVE!

Have the courage to fail forward if necessary. Speak your mind, stick to your values, and accept the consequences. Don't be afraid to tell the truth. Ever. When you are asked if you have an opinion, HAVE ONE! When early in my career I was told, "Errol, your Achilles heel in business is that you have a conscience"; what that meant was that I felt a huge burden to tell the truth no matter how hard it was. After years of reflection, I have come to realize that telling the truth is my greatest strength. It can be hard, especially if you do not have a receptive boss. But if you join a team and expect to be a Yes man or woman, you may need to change teams. Do not compromise your morals for your paycheck.

LESSON 11.2: BRAVERY HAS ITS COSTS

Understand the ramifications of speaking up and be prepared to deal with them. I took a chance when I had an honest conversation with my CEO. At the time, I was four levels below him in the company hierarchy. However, I believed my honesty would be welcomed. In that moment, my words could have just as easily negatively impacted my career. Instead of a promotion, I could have been demoted, or just ended up becoming stagnant in my career. I would have had to accept those consequences for speaking up. Pushing back against the establishment comes with risk. High risk can yield high rewards, but it can also lead to your downfall as well. It is important to be pragmatic in your approach. If you are going to be upfront, honest, and bring something to the attention of your organization, be prepared for the possibility that they may not be receptive to what you say.

What is your Plan B? If you are so dependent on the job that you may regret such actions, you should come up with another tactic. Martyrs are not celebrated in the corporate arena. They can become examples of what not to do in many corporate cultures. It takes wisdom and guts to speak up, but you must also possess the courage to accept the consequences. Make sure you decide with your eyes wide open.

Kate Simpson

Client Account Manager, Big Five accounting firm

"If you don't show your face, and if they don't hear your voice, you can only go so far. You have to be able to speak up and people have to be able to see you and hear you. You can perform the best work in the world, but if you're not a presence in the meetings or on the calls, that's going to prevent you from advancing. You can't just do the work and then send the deliverables and think executives are going to recognize you. Again, you have to be able to be a *presence*. That's how your executives and colleagues will see you as a leader."

CHAPTER 12

Leave Without Burning the Bridge

Your Last 100 Days at a Company Are as Important as Your First 100

If you are always trying to be normal, you will never know how amazing you can be.

—*Maya Angelou*

There is an old story from an unknown author about an elephant and a rope that has always resonated with me. One day, a man passing through an open field in South Africa witnessed a few elephants standing next to one another. They each appeared to be held in place by a small rope, with one end pegged to the ground and the other tied to their front leg. As he walked past them, the man was perplexed about how a colossal, majestic animal could be held by such a small rope. He approached the trainer to ask why these elephants just stood there and never attempted to escape. The trainer explained that years before, when they were babies, he tied them down with a similarly sized rope. Back then, the rope was strong enough to hold their young bodies in place. As they grew up, these elephants came to believe that the rope was still strong enough to hold them in place. Even as adults, despite their size, they never try to break free.

Many of us employees of color in corporate America act like these elephants in our respective work positions. We stay in our positions far too long, with limited or no growth opportunities, minimal annual pay raises, and systemically suffer from stagnant careers. The data show convincingly that we plateau earlier than our White peers. Just like the elephants and their ropes, we too have come to believe we cannot break away and run free. Our jobs are not necessarily holding us down or holding us back. But we have been conditioned to believe that we cannot release ourselves from the job tied around our leg. We've stayed there for years and have been through various experiences and setbacks. We have convinced ourselves there is no reason to test the rope's strength. Maybe it is out of fear; we think

Indira Hector

Global HR Leader, AstraZeneca

"I think when there's either a level of disrespect or you feel that you have no opportunities for advancement. Neither your manager, the manager above them, nor the senior leaders in the organization seem to care. Then it's time to quit."

another company will treat us in the same exact way. Maybe it's out of hopelessness; we tried to break away in the past and failed. So we never muster up the courage to try again. Rather than taking the leap of faith, breaking away, and testing that rope, we stay put. We act demure and reticent. We have come to think that this corporate rope around our leg is more powerful than it really is. This has to stop. Today!

Finding the way up our corporate mountain should become easier over time because of the many who came before us. Think about it. Whenever explorers venture into new terrains, they start by walking through an untouched forest with no footsteps to follow.

As they cut the brush and fight through the forest, they begin to create trails, which will later be used by explorers that follow. Sooner or later those trails become wider and turn into routes. Eventually, these routes become standard modes of travel for many. That is exactly what happens with people of color as they penetrate the upper echelons of leadership. Each person who follows has an easier path to travel as they journey through a slightly less rough terrain. Each generation should see improvement. It should get a little easier. I inherently understand that my path today is easier than that of those who came before me. Yet, I am inspired by the fact that my journey will also make it a little bit easier for the next diverse generation who will climb after me.

However, the statistics tell us a different story. It is still alarming how much diversity at the top ranks of major corporations has remained unchanged over the past 20 years. Based on data from McKinsey & Company, shown in Figure 12.1, the prospect of moving up as an employee of color remains daunting, if not nearly impossible. Additionally, the imbalance for underrepresented professionals starts right at the entry level. However, without the collective power to change things at the top, our key is to focus on the things you can control.

My goal has been to ensure that if and when an opportunity does arise, I am ready to jump on it without any excuses. After all, success is when opportunity meets preparation. But we have to be courageous enough to pursue those opportunities in the first place, or they become moot. And think about this . . . moving up the ranks in corporate America is a team sport for us employees of color. Imagine if just one

The pipeline to highly compensated executive roles sheds professionals of color, especially black professionals, at every level.

Share of professionals by role category, %¹

A Entry-level professional, **B** manager, **C** senior manager/director, **D** vice president, **E** senior vice president, **F** C-suite professional

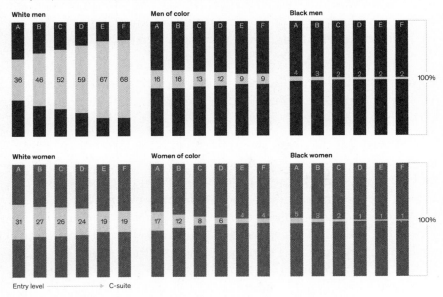

¹From study of 279 North America–focused companies. Figures may not sum to 100%, because of rounding.
Source: *Women in the Workplace 2018*, joint report by LeanIn.Org and McKinsey, October 2018, womenintheworkplace.com

Figure 12.1   The pipeline to highly compensated executive roles sheds professionals of color, especially Black professionals, at every level.
Source: Nick Noel, Duwain Pinder, Shelley Stewart, and Jason Wright, "The Economic Impact of Closing the Racial Wealth Gap," McKinsey & Company, August 13, 2019.

of those elephants standing among their peers tried to pull away from that small rope. Not only would that one elephant be free, but all the other elephants would witness the breakaway and follow suit. But in the workplace, I have often observed the contrary. Rather than testing the rope, we succumb to fear and stay in bondage.

By standing in the same place for so long, our muscles and minds begin to atrophy, and our skills degrade. To put it bluntly, if we are not growing at work, we are slowly dying. But the fear to try something new or leave our current environment is often due to the Sunken Cost Fallacy, which one *Harvard Business Review* article describes as "someone [who] chooses to do or continue something just because they have invested (unrecoverable) resources in it in the past."[1] In the health economics courses that I teach at New York University, my students learn that unrecoverable costs should be disregarded when considering future decisions. That is, even if you lost millions of dollars on an investment, when you are deciding whether or not to close your business, the money spent in previous years should not be factored into your decision. Sunken costs can include money, time, resources, or simply efforts expended.

We should definitely apply this to our careers. Even if you've spent a decade at a company, your past tenure should have no bearing on whether you decide to stay or go. Essentially, it's imperative to cut your losses when deciding your future.

That's precisely why if you wake up and come to the realization that you are either in a dead-end job or you have hit your head on the proverbial glass and/or concrete ceiling, it's time to plan your escape. If you can't fish, cut bait. But before you do, it is important that you have a getaway plan.

Robert Childs

Executive Vice President of Enterprise, Inclusion, Diversity and Business Engagement at American Express

"Know Your Blind Spots. It is important you have confidence and believe in yourself. Too much confidence can cause you to miss some things, real or perceived, that others see which will influence how they assess your potential to advance. Assuming you are asking feedback about the work and progress you are making; revisit the way you ask the question. If you are asking, "How am I doing?" you may get some general answers like "Good," "Okay," or "Not bad." If you accept those answers and move on to another topic, you are missing an opportunity to get meaningful feedback. Consider follow-up probes like "What was so good about it?" or "What would take it from not bad to wow?" Remember the person you report to is in rooms and meetings you are not, so getting their perspective on what works in those rooms are nuggets you should mine as often as you can."

I had worked at the same company for close to a decade. When it was time for me to think about going elsewhere, I knew I could not just leave. I had to prepare myself to depart in a way that did not burn any bridges. I was dutifully intentional about how I left, especially as an employee of color with only one major corporation on my resume. What I have found is that despite our extremely large economy, individual industries can still feel small in size. Many of the executives in your industry have worked at the same subset of companies, meaning relationships (or the lack thereof) can greatly impact which doors of opportunity open. Leaving one of these companies on good terms, especially at higher levels, is key to succeeding in your industry.

You want to keep those doors of opportunity open! Even if you never return to your old company, I guarantee that a new company will most likely have executives who used to work at your previous firm. Your reputation is key, especially with the advent of LinkedIn. Now it is easier than ever for recruiters and hiring managers to see where you worked and with whom. This ubiquitous data mean that now you are not the only person that controls your narrative. Past or present colleagues can weigh in on your performance and significantly impact your reputation—for better or worse.

A 2009 study called "Discrimination in a Low-Wage Market: A Field Experiment" found that Black job applicants were half as likely to get a positive response back from an employer as compared with equally qualified White applicants. Hispanic/Latinx applicants received a positive response 80% of the time as compared to their White peers.[2] The study then gave each race equivalent resumes, yet only White applicants were given criminal records. The White applicants still fared better than Black and Hispanic/Latinx applicants without a record! This seems absurd, but it is backed by evidence. In fact, when people of color are hired, there are times where their role is "channeled down." Despite applying for a sales role position, they get hired as a "stock boy." This type of trend continues for employees of color as we move up the corporate mountain.

Another 2017 study analyzed 28 discrimination research studies from 1989 through 2014 to determine if discrimination in hiring practices decreased over time.[3] The findings were dismal. Since 1989, White applicants received 36% more callbacks than Black applicants, and 24% more than Hispanic/Latino applicants. Even when you control for education, gender, occupation, and conditions in the labor market, the statistics do not get any better. As recently as 2016, the study found that discrimination in hiring at all levels of an organization is still rampant in America.

This was the reality I found myself facing when I sought my next job. I couldn't alter these statistics; I just had to figure out how to maneuver through them. I understood the corporate mountain ahead of me that I needed to climb. The following steps will assist you in your transition.

Step One: I was very intentional about my branding externally. It is better to tell your own story than have a recruiter develop one for you, particularly if they are not likely to see or consider your resume.

To distinguish myself, I developed a personal website to super-charge my branding. My website housed a blog where I wrote about the healthcare industry. I transformed my NYU graduate school health policy papers into updated blog posts. This way, recruiters who looked me up on LinkedIn would find themselves on my website after a few clicks. Most corporations do not have issues with diversity at the lower levels of employment, as the McKinsey data showed earlier. Unfortunately, the hiring of senior leaders and executives of color is subject to much more subjectivity and bias.

For example, it's easy to have very objective criteria for a call center. There are key requirements an employee must have in order to get hired. It is not difficult to ascertain whether a prospective hire has those skills. It's much harder to have the same objectivity for leadership roles. What tends to happen is that executives are hired based on gut feelings, comfort, and the candidate's prior experiences as opposed to tangible metrics that can be measured apples to apples between individuals.

Prior experience is also another downfall for people of color. Because of the lack of diversity in the highest ranks, it is much harder to find executives of color who had prior experience at very senior levels, which is a self-fulfilling prophecy that only furthers the stagnation.

Step Two: I focused on education. For people of color, it's an important puzzle piece for job advancement. That is why I went back to school for my graduate degree in Health Policy and Financial

Management before I left my position. If you are going back to school for a postgraduate degree, your goal should be to find a school within your budget, with enough gravitas that the name alone will speak for itself on your resume. Then pick a versatile program or a degree that will showcase that you learned "in-demand" transferrable skills that make you an asset in multiple departments. Those degrees include law, computer science, finance, accounting, engineering, or math.

In today's environment, companies are focused on big data, analytics, digital transformation, and growth: degrees that speak to your ability to synthesis data, garner insights, and develop strategy. Execution will win the day. If you are choosing between several schools, let the alumni network break the tie. Schools with strong alumni networks that allow you to engage in programs that will support your career growth post graduation should be the deciding factor. The stronger your alumni network, the better chance you'll have getting into a company through a professional referral rather than just submitting a resume online. I have referred, hired, and promoted countless students of color from my alma mater to the companies for which I've worked. It still surprises me how many students of color never reach out to me for opportunities, even after I personally gave my contact information to them. If you ever can engage with alumni from your school who are high ranking in business, do not squander that opportunity. They are there to help you grow professionally. Leverage these relationships and pay it forward later in your career.

When I decided to go back to school, I chose a more expensive school, New York University (NYU), for several reasons, including its name recognition. The timing was also intentional. I was enrolling at the time President Obama was on the verge of passing thelargest, most influential healthcare legislation since 1965: the Affordable Care Act. I knew I was going to have access to nationally renowned professors and a wide-reaching alumni network. In fact, NYU Dean Sherry Glied served as Assistant Secretary of the U.S. Department of Health and Human Services in the Obama administration.[4] Ironically, several years after graduating, I would return to NYU to teach Dean Glied's Health Economics course during the summer of 2020.

I also knew I wanted to stay in New York as I accelerated my career. Becoming a student at NYU immediately expanded my New York metropolitan network to similar professionals in my field. Overnight, I became classmates and friends with other healthcare executives who were eager and willing to accept an email or LinkedIn message from me. All these new connections became friends and resources I could rely upon. I am still close to many of my classmates I met through my master's program, and I often see them personally and professionally.

Step Three: I leveraged my networks. When I was ready to exit, most of the employment opportunities I entertained were not from job postings or career websites. No, the leads and job prospects I mulled over came almost exclusively through personal and professional referrals. The importance and power of networking cannot be overstated. Remember this when you allow nervousness or anxiety to stop you from introducing yourself to an executive at a networking event, Zoom call, or gala. What you are sacrificing is much more than just a shallow introduction. You are giving up the potential for a future opportunity.

> **Kate Simpson**
>
> *Client Account Manager, Big Five accounting firm*
>
> "In this virtual age, still strive to get on people's calendars. Try a walk-and-talk or coffee chat. It doesn't have be on Zoom. It can be very informal. Just 15 minutes. Try to decrease the time required and the formality. Executives and colleagues appreciate that."

Through my network, I began having exploratory conversations with other healthcare companies. That is exactly how an executive of another health insurance company initially heard about me. While he solicited help from his network to recruit new talent into his organization, someone placed my resume in his lap. He reached out via email, and we started a conversation. That turned into several more and soon enough he sent me an offer letter. Numerous job opportunities in corporate America come about in this fashion, through good old-fashioned networking, relationships, and referrals. Once again, it's too late to try to form these bonds when you're making your exit. The key is to form them before you're in need.

Step Four: I nurtured my resume. Your resume is the first glimpse for a company to understand who you are and what you bring to the table. That's why it's crucial to maintain your resume as a living and breathing document. It should be continually updated. Keep it on your desktop and refresh it on an ongoing basis as you complete new projects at work. Turn it into a *real-time resume*.

Too many of us only pull our resume off a dusty shelf to update when we are desperately seeking a job. However, if you move into the mindset that your resume is for YOU and not for THEM, then you treat it like a houseplant.

Yes, you read this right. A houseplant. Indulge me for a moment.

Water it. A plant constantly needs watering, which provides nutrients so that it can grow. You don't starve a plant until it turns brown, shrivels up, and is about to die before pouring a gallon of water on it. However, that is how most of us handle our resumes. We leave them static, lying around, and starving for new and relevant information. We should update them regularly in real time based on our accomplishments.

One of the benefits of a *real-time resume* is that it makes it easier to recall quantifiable results with exact figures. Putting those figures into your resume when they are fresh in your mind is a great way to record your work achievements. Waiting to update your resume until you are applying for a job will make it much harder to remember those KPIs (Key Performance Indicators) or metrics that made your work successful.

Prune it. You prune plants by cutting and removing their old leaves and stems, which makes room for new ones to grow. Resumes should be updated in the exact same fashion. Your entry-level job can be reduced to one or two lines on your resume as you move into middle management and have more years under your belt. Your current job should have much more information and details.

As your career advances, your resume can grow in length. With less than five years of experience, your resume should easily fit into one page. A rule of thumb has been once you've reached 10 or more years of experience, you can extend the resume to a second page, but the most recent experiences should take up much of the space.

Give it light. You need to ensure that your plant has sufficient light, which is an essential fuel for growth. Indeed, without light, a plant will not grow. Similarly, you should share your resume with those in your inner circle for them to proof-read, analyze, and give you constructive feedback. If a resume stays hidden in the dark for too long, it will not grow and bloom as much as it would have if it was exposed to others. Sharing your resume with mentors or colleagues will only strengthen it.

Pot it. Finally, you must think about the soil and the pot into which you will place your plant. The soil has the nutrients that help nourish a plant. Soil also helps to anchor a plant so it can grow strong roots and stand tall. Think of the soil as the company where you work. Does your company invest in you with development programs and other activities that improve your professional skills? Is your company offering you a strong foundation to build and grow a career successfully? These are key questions you'll have to ask yourself.

I remember coaching Anthony with this amusing plant analogy a few years ago. He was a mid-level employee in corporate America who reached out for my help on LinkedIn. Anthony was an African American male, who, like many, was the first of his family to go to college. I met him through the mentoring work I do at my alma mater, Fordham University. His resume was filled with very esoteric bullet points that lacked specificity. For example, he would write, "As a lead project coordinator, I supported key initiatives and kept teams organized." These types of bland statements do not stand out to recruiters and hiring managers. Can you imagine how many resumes they see each day? They see these same words and descriptions over and over again.

After working with me, Anthony improved his resume with more distinctive and quantifiable sentences. Now his position was described as:

Project Coordinator

- Led timely and impactful project meetings that facilitated the successful launch of the company's new website.
- The website was released on time without defects, and subsequent page visits grew by 32% post launch.
- Responsible for all aspects of the project, identifying important next steps, facilitating meetings, and informing senior stakeholders about key decisions on a timely basis.
- As a result of these efforts, the initiative stayed ahead of schedule and under budget by $40,000. Various business leaders have since recruited me to lead newer initiatives based on project results.

This level of detail stands out. While it is important to not be verbose, it is imperative to articulate what value you can bring to an organization. Outlining tangible metrics and value creation in a resume is key for making the best first impression. Often, our resume precedes us. Indeed, it is our first impression!

After updating his resume, Anthony applied for a position internally and was hired as a Project Director. Anthony was able to exit *and* ascend. May we all be as blessed when we are prepared to leave.

LESSON 12.1: SET YOUR OWN CLOCK

It's important to control your own destiny. As tempting and comfortable as it may sound, do not let corporate America set your clock. Take the onus upon yourself to set it yourself. A boss once told me to "wait" for a promotion. He convinced me that it would take five years to reach the next level of my career. I have heard so many stories of people waiting in the wings for a promotion that had only been discussed in vague, esoteric ways, lacking any concrete timelines, specifics, or guarantees. Do not build future plans on a foundation of sand. If you're told to wait for a promotion, but in your heart of hearts you believe it's long overdue, then find a way to chase your dream. It is okay to leave an organization when it is warranted. Often, we feel an artificial connection to a company because of the years we've served. Do not fall into that trap. Don't let your past pollute your future. You must make the best decision for your career and your family. Be impatient with your dreams and demanding of your place in the world. Don't hang your hopes on so-called promises from a company unwilling to paint a full picture of your future.

LESSON 12.2: THE TOP 10 "DO's" OF LEAVING ON GOOD TERMS

I have counseled many mentees and colleagues of color about the importance of leaving an organization in the right way. Here are the top 10 "Do's" to dwell on:

1. **Do:** Type out a letter of resignation. Email it to your boss and give him or her a hard copy (in person if possible). With Zoom calls and working remotely, this could be much harder.

2. **Do:** Thank your boss, your team, and the company for the opportunity to learn and work at the firm. Do also acknowledge the positive experiences you've had while working in your role.

3. **Do:** Tell your boss first thing in the morning. Politely ask to speak with him or her as the day starts, make eye contact, thank your boss for the opportunity, and let him or her know that you are resigning as of today.

4. **Do:** Have a date in mind and include that date in your resignation letter. Industry standard is two weeks. That is the bare minimum. I have always given more time. Anything less could be seen as leaving on bad terms. If possible, plan for more than two weeks. It is a sign of respect to both your boss and the company. The higher up you go, the more time you

should give. Do not take paid time off during the period of time that you gave notice.

5. **Do:** Offer up a transition plan. Prior to leaving, organize a list of all the projects you are working on with progress reports and key next steps. Identify who on the team can potentially take them over based on your recommendation and assessment. In the past, I have set up a shared folder with all of my notes and key documents that are essential to the transition plan. Helping your boss get his or her arms around your work is a nice way of leaving cordially and setting up your boss for success.

6. **Do:** Be prepared to leave on the spot. It might happen, especially if you are going to a competitor. While it may be uncomfortable, let your boss know which company you are heading to (you can ask your boss to keep it confidential if you so choose). If you are going to a competitor, make sure you double-check whether you have a noncompete clause or a nondisclosure agreement. It is important to be cognizant of any rules or guidelines you agreed to before resigning.

7. **Do:** Know how you will answer if you are asked to stay or are given a counteroffer. You may be asked by your boss to change your decision. You may even be asked for a salary amount that would be enough to change your mind about quitting. You could even be promised a promotion! Make sure you know the answers to these questions before they are asked. Resign without regrets. If there are conditions that would convince you to stay, clearly articulate them right then and there. Do your boss a favor and have this hashed out in your mind prior to your potential discussion. Dragging out a resignation only makes it more convoluted and stressful for all parties involved.

8. **Do:** Realize that if you have already resigned and given a verbal acceptance to another company, it is best to see that decision through. Whatever has taken place that compelled you to resign will not magically be resolved with a new title or more money. The Society of Human Resource

Management found that nearly 60% of employees who accept a counteroffer leave the company within 24 months.[5] Counteroffers are short-term fixes that manifest into long-term problems.

9. **Do:** Make sure you properly say goodbye to your colleagues and offer to keep in touch with them, especially any close friends, mentors, or allies you've made along the way. Do share your contact information with your key contacts. Also, think about sending a note saying goodbye, but "BCC" everyone, which is just corporate email etiquette to avoid starting an email trail that will never end.

10. **Do:** Take some time off before starting your new position. It is healthy to give yourself some time to decompress and recharge your batteries before starting your new role. You want to give yourself the best runway for starting the new role successfully. Give your body and brain the time and separation they require before jumping into something brand new. Afford yourself the grace to fully close one book before opening another.

CHAPTER 13

Exude Executive Presence

*How to Flourish as a Leader of Color
on Your Way Up the Corporate Mountain*

In the past, power was centralized in the hands of the few people who had access to information. Now that information is available everywhere, the leader's critical question is "How do I charge up the organization so that we're maximizing the intellect of all of our people?"

—*Bernard Tyson, former President and CEO, Kaiser Permanente*

Bernard Tyson was one of the most influential healthcare executives in America. As a child, Bernard decided he wanted to run his own hospital after seeing his mother consistently being hospitalized due to her never-ending struggle with diabetes. He went back to school for his MBA to gain more knowledge and master his craft. He started as an administrative analyst at Vallejo General Hospital in 1981 and later became the CEO of Kaiser Foundation Hospital in Santa Rosa, California by 1992. He was 33 years old.

Bernard Tyson found the way up the corporate mountain to a corner office in just 11 years! Upon assuming an executive position, he is quoted as saying, "I thought I had arrived—I never thought it would only last for a year." That is because he quickly got promoted within Kaiser Permanente to even larger roles: Senior Vice President (1999–2006), Executive Vice President (2006–2010), President and Chief Operating Officer (2010–2013), and finally Chairman and Chief Executive Office from 2014[1] until his untimely death on November 10, 2019. In addition, Kaiser Permanente renamed its School of Medicine after Bernard Tyson in honor of his passing. Despite his death, his legacy of leadership will live on, especially in those he inspired like me. To this day, I still glean lessons of leadership from the stories I read about him. He is an exemplary shining light of executive presence.

Bernard Tyson's story resonated with me on so many levels. When I became the Chief Operating Officer of one of the largest health insurance companies in New York, I too was a Black executive in my early thirties. I too worked for a subsidiary of a much larger organization. And I would also remain in this role for about a year as well. *There were so many parallels*. Mr. Tyson soon became someone I would emulate as a Black executive in healthcare. As the founder of the Children's

Defense Fund, Marian Wright Edelman, said, "You can't see what you can't be." Well, when I started my career in healthcare, I saw Mr. Tyson. I saw him exude executive presence in all of his interviews, public statements, and community outings. He was more than just a CEO; he was a giant. And now that I was a Black executive, I aspired to be him.

Back then, when I did not drive into Manhattan for work, I would take the BxM8 express bus from The Bronx to arrive in lower Manhattan. The bus route would speed down 5th Avenue, and once we approached West 51st Street, I would lean over to briefly gaze upon a 45-foot, seven-ton bronze statue of Atlas. Created by Lee Lawrie and Rene Paul Chambellan, the statue stood tall and proud every single morning in front of Rockefeller Center, while staring at St. Patrick's Cathedral across the street.

At first glance of this muscular man holding the world on his shoulders, I always thought the statue conveyed strength and stability. However, after some careful research, I discovered that it depicts Atlas's punishment rather than his powers. Years earlier, he led an army of Titans into a failed war against the Olympian gods with the goal of controlling the heavens and Earth. As punishment, Zeus banished him and forced him to hold up those same heavens and Earth for the rest of eternity.

You may not believe it, but becoming a C-Suite executive felt quite similar. While my title and position in the company projected strength and confidence, I too felt punished for trying to reach the top echelons of my company. It felt audacious. At times, I was uncomfortable wondering if I was indeed *too big for my britches*. I would soon discover how lonely it is at the top. I was consumed by the responsibilities of my new position. In many ways, my promotion felt more like I was holding up the weight of the world all by myself.

I had over 1,500 direct and indirect employees looking to me for leadership and vision. I understood that hundreds of them complained about their boss or their company to their spouses every night. I realized that these complaints were often based on the hundreds of decisions I had to make. Some of these decisions were excruciating in that they led to layoffs and job losses. I recall often waking up in the middle of the night thinking about decisions that had to be made later that

Robert Childs

Executive Vice President of Enterprise, Inclusion, Diversity and Business Engagement at American Express

"While I recognize racism, bias, and close-minded thinking exists, I treat them like just one more set of hurdles in the way toward a bigger outcome. I focus my energy on building resilience and getting to know people on a level where both of us can find some commonality in desired outcomes and some shared values. When someone crosses a line, I tell them. We talk about it and agree to not repeat certain things. . . . In my opinion, to change the trajectory of bias and discrimination where more inclusion occurs will require individuals to be able to interact with one another to focus more on what they have in common versus focusing on the things which are different. Science has shown that human beings have 99.9% of the same DNA, yet we are divided by less than 0.1%, which is amplified by the bubbles we grow up in and sadly choose to remain in."

same day. My dreams were consumed with the consequences of my actions.

Walking on Wall Street toward the office under those towering skyscrapers felt almost claustrophobic. Lucky for me, I had worked at this company for close to a decade before returning as the Chief Operating Officer. Having a track record of success, experience, and relationships with key colleagues was crucial. Despite these realities, however, I still walked into the role with insecurities, reservations, and a strong dose of imposter syndrome.

The traumatic reality of growing up in a country steeped in historical racial discrimination is that sometimes you see things that are not always there. Other times, they are there, but you're the only one who can see them.

The confounding and perplexing thing about racism is that it is beyond the control of the victim. It does not matter how smart they are, how hard they work, or how successful they are in their career—at the end of the day, they can change neither the color of their skin nor the hearts and minds of those perpetrating the discrimination. This has the effect of making us feel helpless.

I'd be lying if I said that as an executive of color, it doesn't cross my mind from time to time to ponder if my skin color plays a factor in how I am treated in the workplace. I intentionally repress wondering if I got this role because I deserved it . . . or to fill a quota. While I could not be a stronger proponent of diversity, there does exist a thin line between that and tokenism.

Let me provide an example from Wall Street. On August 6, 2021, Nasdaq's Board Diversity Rule was approved by the Securities and Exchange Commission (SEC). The rule sought to establish a minimum threshold of diversity on the boards of the roughly 3,000 Nasdaq-listed companies. The rule required Nasdaq-listed companies "to have at least two diverse directors, including one woman and one underrepresented minority or described as LGBTQ+."[2] Board diversity reporting would be required annually, and companies that could not meet the minimum standard would have to disclose their reasons why. While this rule was a step in the right direction, Nasdaq also clearly stated that the rule was not a mandate and any reasons for missing the standard would not be reviewed or evaluated. This was yet another diversity rule without teeth!

The goal for these types of policies is to encourage diversity, one would hope, solely for the sake of diversity. Tokenism, as defined by Merriam-Webster, is "the policy or practice of making only a symbolic

Lucy M. Lopez

General Counsel and Chief Legal Officer at Spencer Stuart, a leading global executive search and leadership advisory firm

"DE&I efforts have to be real and sustainable, with authentic leadership. You must have the right people at the table, cross sections of diversity, which includes people of color, different genders, sexual orientations, the underrepresented, diversity of thought, etc., so that you can draw from reality. The best problem-solving will not emerge from a conference room with colleagues who lack personal experience. You need many voices to have the candid and difficult conversations you will need to have. What can we do here? How do we shape something that can work? How do we convince the naysayers in this institution, and those who might feel threatened, to get behind this? I do think it starts with ensuring that you have the right voices in the room from the outset."

effort." A study in 2020 found that 75% of the Nasdaq-listed firms did not meet the requirement.[3] So the question is, which is worse? A Nasdaq-listed company that does not meet the new guidelines and expresses their rationale on their website? Or a company that does meet the guidelines with a slate of diverse board of directors purely as a political or symbolic gesture? I would argue the latter. One of the most subtle but insidious consequences of tokenism is the inability to distinguish between those people who advance through merit from those who serve as symbolic hires offered up to convince us all that America's race problem has been solved.

Ironically, these are not new issues. The National Football League (NFL) tackled this same exact issue back in 2002. A highly successful Black football coach, Tony Dungy, first assumed the head coaching job of the Tampa Bay Buccaneers in 1996. In his first season, the team had a 1-8 win-loss record. However, Coach Dungy began to infuse his leadership onto the team and develop a new defensive scheme dubbed the *Tampa 2*. The team would end the season with a 6-10 record. Tony Dungy would finish the next season in 1997 with a 10-6 record, culminating in the first winning season and playoff appearance for the Bucs since 1982. Two years later, Dungy's 1999 Bucs would finish with an 11-5 record and win the NFC Central Division Championship.

For the next two seasons, Dungy's Tampa Bay Buccaneers would enjoy winning seasons and make the playoffs. But the coveted Super Bowl win remained elusive. Despite completely turning around the Buccaneer's franchise and transforming the culture of the players in the process, Tony Dungy was fired in 2001. The firing of one Black pro football coach, while surprising, did not spark much controversy at the time. What made the news was another Black coach being fired as well!

From 1992 to 2001, Dennis Green served as the head coach of the Minnesota Vikings. Green was the second Black coach in NFL history. During his NFL tenure, Green had one of the best win-loss records. The Vikings never had a losing season from 1992, when Green started, through 2001. Yet, in 2001, with one game left in the season, Dennis Green was the second Black coach to be fired.

The firing of these two competent and successful coaches led to an investigation by two prominent American civil rights attorneys.

They wondered if there was something unscrupulous about these firings, if there was a certain pattern of behavior taking place within the NFL. One of the attorneys leading the fight was Cyrus Mehri, an Iranian American attorney best known as co-counsel in a monumental lawsuit against the Coca-Cola Company.

Cyrus Mehri knew that this case would not be won by appealing to the hearts of people. Rather, he needed hard facts and statistics that supported his claim of alleged disparities in pay and advancement. Mehri would end up joining forces with Johnnie Lee Cochran, Jr., another renowned civil rights attorney, best known for his successful criminal defense and acquittal of O.J. Simpson.[4]

Mehri and Cochran used statistics from all NFL coaches broken down by race in a landmark report reviewing 15 seasons of data called, "Black Coaches in the National Football League: Superior Performance, Inferior Opportunities."[5] Using a credentialed labor economist from the University of Pennsylvania, Dr. Janice Madden, the two attorneys unveiled the staggering statistics they uncovered. Here are a few representative highlights:

- Black NFL coaches averaged 1.1 more wins per season than White coaches.

- Black coaches led their teams to the playoffs 67% of the time compared with 39% of the time for White coaches.

- In their first seasons, Black coaches averaged 2.7 more wins than White coaches in their premier seasons.

- Black coaches inherited teams with an average of 7.4 wins per season and during their tenures increased average wins to 9.1 per season.

All in all, the groundbreaking report showed what Black coaches already knew: there was a higher expectation for them as NFL football coaches, and that they were generally the "last hired and the first fired." Not only was the bar always raised higher for Black coaches, but there was less grace and patience given to them in the face of adversity. In fact, by 2002, when the report was written, there had only been five Black head coaches since 1986: Art Shell, Dennis Green, Tony Dungy,

Ray Rhodes, and Herman Edwards. While Cochran's most famous quip, "If it doesn't fit, you must acquit" proved successful for the O.J. Simpson case, Cochran had another memorable quote when it came to the hiring practices of the NFL. At a news conference following this report, Cochran exclaimed, "You only litigate after you've done everything you can to negotiate."[6]

The news and the fanfare finally pressured the NFL into action. By December 20 of that year, the NFL publicly released their plan to promote diversity in hiring practices. It formed the NFL Committee on Workplace Diversity, which was chaired by one of the most respected NFL owners at the time, Dan Rooney, of the Pittsburgh Steelers. Dan Rooney was the perfect choice, as his family had a history of breaking color barriers. His father, Art Rooney, had brought in the league's first Black player, Ray Kemp, in 1933.[7] In 1969, Dan Rooney would also overcome racial barriers and hire African American Bill Nunn to lead scouting activities for the Pittsburgh Steelers to leverage Nunn's extensive network of relationships with historically Black colleges.[8] At the time, there were very few African American scouts in the league. Rooney's action sent a clear message.

As Chair of the Workplace Diversity Committee in 2002, Dan Rooney led the efforts to implement a diversity plan that included the requirement that each football team interview at least one candidate of color *prior* to selecting a head coach. The rule would later be known as the Rooney Rule.[9]

In the following years, the rule seemed to work. The Pittsburgh Steelers themselves led by example in hiring their own Black coach, Mike Tomlin, in 2007. Mike continues to be their head coach today. Merely five years after the Rooney Rule was inaugurated, history was made: for the first time ever, two Black coaches competed against each other at the Super Bowl. Super Bowl XLI hosted Tony Dungy's Indianapolis Colts and Lovie Smith's Chicago Bears. This was only made possible by the litigated change in hiring practices by the NFL. And remember, these changes did not arise out of charity but instead were based on 15 years of the NFL's own statistics.

By 2017, there were eight Black NFL coaches at the start of the season, tying the record for the most of any season ever. However, this historic moment occurred the same year as Dan Rooney's death. Unfortunately, it seems that the NFL's push for racial equality departed with him. The more things change, the more things stay the same.

As of 2022, there are only two Black head coaches. Just recently, a well-regarded Black coach, Brian Flores, was fired as head coach of the Miami Dolphins after just three seasons by their controversial billionaire owner, Stephen Ross. In an uncanny resemblance to Tony Dungy's tenure with the Tampa Bay Bucs, Brian Flores followed up a losing first season with a winning second season, although making the playoffs proved elusive. In his third and final season, Flores led the Dolphins to a 9-8 record, winning their last seven games of the year.

Days after being fired, Flores filed a class-action lawsuit against the NFL, the New York Giants, the Denver Broncos, and the Miami Dolphins, alleging racial discrimination. Three days before his upcoming interview for the head coaching job at the New York Giants, Flores received text messages from his former boss, Bill Belichick of the New England Patriots, who congratulated him on getting hired. Belichick would later apologize for sending the message, texting, "Sorry—I fucked this up. I double checked and misread the text. I think they are naming Brian Daboll. I'm sorry about that. BB."[10] But that was precisely the moment Flores knew the job had already been given to a White candidate before a candidate of color was interviewed—defiantly breaking the Rooney Rule!

Brian Flores incorporated screenshots of his text exchanges with Belichick in his lawsuit as well. He had the courage to call out bias and discrimination when he saw it. In a show of good faith and grace, the Pittsburgh Steelers announced weeks later that they had hired Brian Flores as their new senior defense assistant and linebackers coach. The opportunity came out of a call requesting advice from that same head coach of the Pittsburgh Steelers, Mike Tomlin. As Flores recounted, "I actually was calling Coach T. to really to get some counsel. I was thinking about the next steps for me just from a coaching standpoint. And then that conversation turned into an opportunity there in Pittsburgh."[11]

Now, what does racism in professional football have to do with racism in corporate America, one may ask? Everything! The NFL owners are a perfect microcosm of the boards of directors for most

Fortune 500 companies across America. The demographics are certainly similar. In 2020, Deloitte released a report showcasing the diversity of the boards of directors for Fortune 500 companies. The largest increase in representation was seen with White women, who had gained 21% more board seats since 2018. Also, the same pool of one third of the diverse board members sit on other Fortune 500 boards—indicating that while diversity is expanding, the actual number of diverse board members are not.[12] Clearly, opportunities are confined to a small number of board members of color. We are not growing the pie.

Even more problematic, women of color continue to remain the most underrepresented at the board level, representing only 5.7% of the board seats as of 2020.

The realities of upper-level management in football or corporate America can be discouraging for people of color trying to interview for these higher-level positions. As the underrepresented class, we are already skeptical of the fairness of the recruitment process. We also do not want to waste our time, efforts, and resources interviewing for positions when these decisions have already been made. We feel like screaming out: "Do not use us to reach your window dressing metrics!"

This concept hit home for me during the COVID-19 pandemic. In an effort to diversify their boards in the wake of the murder of George Floyd, quite a few companies and executive search firms

333	694	1,226	3,627
5.7%	11.8%	20.9%	61.7%
Minority women	Minority men	White women	White men

Fortune 500 companies have shown slower progress creating equitable representation for women and minorities in the boardroom compared with the Fortune 100. Since the first year data was collected for the Fortune 500 (2010), the rate of change continues to increase (from 3.2% from 2016 to 2018 to 4.3% from 2018 to 2020).

Figure 13.1 2020 Fortune 500 percentage of board seats by gender and minority status.
Source: Alliance for Board Diversity, "Missing Pieces Report: The Board Diversity Census of Women and Minorities on Fortune 500 Boards," 6th edition, Deloitte, 2020.

reached out to solicit me for board positions. As the email and LinkedIn messages grew in number, I first felt honored and surprised. I quickly reached out to my mentors to garner advice on how best to interview for such a substantial role. I had to loop in my own boss in the process to ensure that there were not any conflicts of interest and verify that I could manage the time commitment. This was a big deal. Some interviews went several rounds with a myriad of people, while others never moved past the initial call from the recruiter. The number-one question posed to me was about my relevant board experience. While I have presented to boards and have been a member of several nonprofit boards, a for-profit board seat would be a first for me. Ironically, that seemed to be my biggest impediment. A bit of circular reasoning to expand diversity while they look for diverse talent *with prior experience*, which leads to throwaway comments like, "We could not find any credible or qualified candidates of color." It also explains why the Deloitte study discussed earlier found that many Fortune 500 companies tap the same people of color for their various board seats.

Sachin H. Jain, MD, MBA

Recognized by Modern Healthcare magazine *as one of America's 100 most influential leaders in healthcare*

"At one company, there was a biased manager who claimed that they tried to find diverse candidates and just couldn't. To that I say, "How are you looking? Where are you looking? What is your definition of talent? How can you broaden your lens? How can you take risks in helping people to be successful?" I think a lot of the workaround trying to improve diversity of the American corporate workforce is an exercise in insanity. What Einstein called insanity: "Doing the same exact thing and expecting different results." As soon as you start to pivot at it, you can find a lot of great talent if you just decide to. When they say dumb things is when you realize that they're not really as sincerely committed as they may think they are. . . . Any time you get a group that is too lopsided to one kind of person, the outcomes are always worse than when you have a group of people who were joined by similar values, but have also had different experiences. What you're really looking for from diversity is to enrich decision-making. Positive diversity is when more voices lead to more thoughtful decisions and better outcomes for the organization."

I tried to picture the diversity of the nominating committee and thought about their discussions. I could not help but wonder if I was seriously being considered as a board member or if I was helping to meet some metric or quota. I also wondered about whom they ended up selecting. Despite my many interviews during the summer and fall months of 2020, I never did land a board seat. Was I involved in any meaningless interviews like Brian Flores, to simply support symbolic or tokenistic gestures?

And in the small percentage of a chance a person of color or a woman does get the big role at the top, the next riddle to solve is whether the role was given as a "glass cliff assignment." Lynn Perry Wooten has studied this phenomenon and found that African American CEOs disproportionately gain their leadership roles during times of crisis or needed cleanup.[13]

As employees of color in corporate America, you will likely stumble upon the concept of *Performative Allyship*, which runs rampant throughout organizations that attempt to do the right thing while being scared to upset the apple cart. Fortune describes Performative Allyship as those companies that publicly declare their support for marginalized employee populations, yet their words are not backed up by true, authentic actions.[14] Actions that seek to identify the root causes of bias and commit to real improvements that are specific, measurable, and time-bound. Talking the talk *and* walking the walk.

Performative allyship can appear in a variety of ways in corporate America. The leadership may launch Employee Affinity Groups, but not adequately support them with financial resources, executive sponsorship, or governance. It could also look like protecting influential people within the company from punishment despite their visible reluctance to advance racial or gender equality. It is the failure to face the elephant in the room when discrimination or bias happens. It looks like big-dollar pledges to non-profits outside of the company to support communities of color, while pay inequities continue to persist within the four walls of that same company.

It can also feel like the corporate support for underrepresented employees is disingenuous, which can have grave consequences. Employees of color can misinterpret these gestures of perceived allyship and go out on the

Stanley E. Grayson

Board Member of TD Bank, N.A. and Mutual of America Investment Corporation

"You can't keep going to the same places, to the same schools, to the same organizations and expect a different result. I think corporate America is starting to realize that there are certainly more resources today than, you know, three, four or ten years ago."

limb to call out discrimination or bias in their company. Yet in these moments of reckoning, often their so-called allies will cower in fear instead of stepping up to fight. The outcome is usually that difficult issues are swept under the rug rather than being challenged head-on.

Once employees of color learn that this allyship is performative and disingenuous, they shut down. In turn, diversity, equity, and inclusion (DE&I) activities become mere shells of what they could've been. This is why DE&I efforts often fail. It seems clear that the initial goal was never to change the status quo. When an organization gets to a point where their DE&I initiatives are a skeleton of what they once were, that's when the negative reactions occur. Undoubtedly, someone will ask, "Why do we have these programs in the first place?" At which point, the company may conclude that such efforts are not an efficient use of anyone's time, money, or resources. Or that the inequity issue they were originally trying to solve has been fixed! And just like the NFL and the Rooney Rule, the company will be right back to where it started.

The failure of DE&I programs to improve diversity in the workplace has been well researched by experts like Pamela Newkirk, the author of *Diversity, Inc: The Failed Promise of a Billion-Dollar Business*, who discusses the Rooney Rule and the Coca-Cola case extensively.

I too have seen this occur in corporate America. A company's actions can often be subtle, silent, and insidious. First, it starts with you not being invited to meetings that impact your area. Next, you receive performance reviews that are based on subjective and nebulous criteria. The boss may say something like, "I cannot quite put my finger on it, but Jim seems to take more time than necessary to form his ideas and gain alignment." Vague platitudes are used to block you from advancing, yet the feedback is too indistinct for you to actually act on it.

Throughout my career, I have witnessed numerous instances of a company going out of its way to salvage an employee who is not in the right position and is underperforming. Usually, those employees are not employees of color. In my humble experience, bosses tend to have sympathy and empathy for employees who remind them of themselves. They will often try to find their subordinates a new home within the organization. For employees of color, the possibility of having a similar champion within the company is rare. Due to the lack of diversity at the top of most organizations, employees of color can find it difficult to latch onto a support system. As such, it can feel like the organization has less patience with them. They get cast aside more often—just like coaches in the NFL.

I recall Cecilia, an Afro-Latina who was hired into my organization. She was among five other credible candidates who made it to the final round for in-person interviews. The slate of candidates ranged in experience, age, industry background, and ethnicity. We soon determined that Cecilia was the most qualified candidate. I was excited for her to hear the news. Cecilia was equally enthused and made it a point to tell me that she wouldn't let me down. She realized that I was going out on a limb to hire her.

Unfortunately, Cecilia got off to a rocky start. A few of her early projects were not handled with the best of care. In addition, she was reluctant to raise her hand and ask for help to avoid being perceived as weak or incompetent. She even felt uncomfortable asking me for help, even though we had weekly one-on-one meetings. Eventually, we had to have a heart-to-heart conversation where I candidly stated that I was there to support her, but she had to keep me in the loop on issues so I could help her navigate within the organization. The goal was to find her some quick wins.

Cecilia's behavior sadly did not change, and the negative feedback only grew and grew. She had taken on a position that required extensive improvement. However, I could feel her impatience on how slow things were turning around. Cecilia was not given time to have a learning curve or to understand her role. After six months, my leadership team was already contemplating corrective action.

Cecilia was shocked at the news. She raised concerns regarding racial bias among her

Robert Childs

Executive Vice President of Enterprise, Inclusion, Diversity and Business Engagement at American Express

"You will rarely know the full story. While bias exists, it is easy to conclude why one person got the opportunity and the other did not. Absence any facts, the mind fills that vacuum with guesses and assumptions. Those assumptions can fester into resentment and other negative feelings. In my 35+ years, the decision was far less a racial bias and more about the importance of establishing a sense of comfort through relationship people. Finding the points of commonality versus focusing on what makes us different."

peers. Yet, there was much ambiguity in her accusations since the focus stayed on "tone" and "condescension." Derogatory or discriminatory words were never actually said. However, Cecilia responded with hostility to the words and phrases she perceived as racially charged. This made the situation untenable. Regardless of how you feel, reacting emotionally in the moment only muddies up the waters.

One of the hardest conversations I ever had was speaking with Cecilia moments after her termination. With the help of HR, there was a well-documented case that her performance and ability to mesh with the company culture was not meeting the minimum requirements. By the time Cecilia exited the company, she had alienated her peers, including her colleagues of color. As a champion, I was saddened. I felt like I had let her down. Without substantiated claims of discrimination, it was hard for her boss and her support group to help her navigate the situation internally. Without anything more than anecdotes and unsubstantiated claims of bias, Cecilia came across as an underperforming employee who was now using race as an excuse. Once that message took hold, all efforts to rectify the situation or rehabilitate her reputation were futile.

Looking back, I think about what I could have done to further help Cecilia. I want to stop similar circumstances from happening to future employees of color. I now realize that more work needed to be done during Cecilia's onboarding to ensure her success. Similar to the treatment of Black NFL coaches, does corporate America have higher expectations for executives or color? In my experience, over the past 18 years in corporate America, I believe the answer is unequivocally yes.

As an executive of color, it is imperative to keep your executive presence intact as you navigate the higher expectation levels, the lower levels of patience for mediocrity, and a team of employees looking for leadership. The following are four key rules of the road to ensure that you continue to cast a wide leadership shadow.

LESSON 13.1: CREATE AN ENVIRONMENT FOR THRIVERS

As an executive, your number-one job is to create an environment for your teams to thrive. This includes everyone in your organization, including the underrepresented employees. As Bernard Tyson stated in the quote earlier in this chapter, your goal is to maximize the talent of your teams. People do not always remember who has the right answer, but they never forget how another person made them *feel*. Healthy, inclusive work environments that foster belonging are created by curating a deliberate corporate culture. In a *Harvard Business Review* article, Bryan Walker and Sarah A. Soule describe corporate culture as: "The wind. It is invisible, yet its effect can be seen and felt. When it is blowing in your direction, it makes for smooth sailing. When it is blowing against you, everything is more difficult."[15] In my opinion, the most important attributes of strong corporate culture are autonomy, transparency in decision-making, integrity, inclusion, belonging, and teamwork.

LESSON 13.2: PROVIDE A COMPELLING AND INSPIRATIONAL VISION

A vision is what holds a company together. It is the reason why a NASA janitor felt like he was helping to put a man on the moon when President John F. Kennedy visited Cape Canaveral in 1962. A vision is motivational and allows employees to rally around something bigger than themselves. When your employees can link their job to the vision and mission of the company, you unleash the full power and potential of your team.

Your vision should also include your DE&I goals. Grand visions about the company's size and revenue in five to 10 years should also include setting goals around diversity, especially in the higher ranks. Companies have a habit of shooting for exceptional business goals without including targets that inspire and include the company culture. For example, if a company's CEO aims for zero emissions by 2030 as a climate change goal, but fails to describe the makeup of the company that will get them there, they miss an opportunity to declare a clear vision on diversity. Imagine if that same CEO shares that same goal, but also states that the team that will achieve this will be the most diverse group of employees ever seen at their company. Imagine if they set climate targets that will be met by a board of directors where a third are underrepresented racial and ethnic employees of color!

A CEO needs to put money on the line to further confirm the

> **Indira Hector**
>
> *Global HR Leader, AstraZeneca*
>
> "A DE&I department is effective when there's senior leader partnership and the leaders really want to make a change in the organization. When they truly believe in diversity and want to diversify the organization. That they are really holding themselves to account and it really is in their goals and objectives to annually hire a certain percentage of minorities. If they don't, than it affects their bonus. I think when there are dedicated resources with true strategies that link to business results, we see a lot more impact. Very few companies are willing to go there. So most of these strategies fail."

seriousness of the diversity goals of the company. We are now seeing more and more organizations including diversity targets as part of their annual and long-term incentive programs for the senior leaders. Putting these leaders' wallets at risk is another way to hold an organization accountable for this important work. The achievement of these goals should affect their salaries and bonuses! Combining business consequences with diversity goals is the next evolution for corporations in a post-George Floyd world.

LESSON 13.3: HONOR YOUR FIDUCIARY RESPONSIBILITIES

It is imperative that as an executive you live and breathe the phrase "there is no mission without margin." Ensuring the longevity of your company and all the employees you are privileged to serve starts with financial discipline. You must make the hard decisions that ensure the survival of your firm. If your firm prospers, the lives within that firm can prosper. To me, that is your highest calling.

Within the realm of financial discipline is pay equity. Employees performing similar duties with the same tenure and experience should be paid equally, or at least similarly. Will there be slight differences in pay? Absolutely! And there should be, particularly if pay is merit-based. However, grave disparities exceeding 30%–40% differentials are inexcusable. Without considering education level, job type, or experience, on average a woman earns $0.82 for every $1 earned by a White man, dropping to $0.79 for Black women and $0.78 for Hispanic/Latina women. These differences amount to hundreds of thousands of dollars in lower pay for women of color over their lifetime, which directly impacts their ability to provide for their families.

These problems do not become equitable the higher you move up. With similar education and experience, women executives still only earn 95% of what a White man earns in the same exact role. At a compensation level of $250,000 for a White male executive, a female executive would earn $237,500, which, over the course of a 40-year career, can mean a shortfall of half a million dollars!

Companies can no longer allow this pay inequity to persist at their firms. There is a fiduciary responsibility for a firm to compensate their employees fairly for work that is done.

LESSON 13.4: PRACTICE SELF-CARE

If you can't care for yourself, how will you be able to care for others? This can be understood by thinking about your basic airline flight. When they review the safety procedures, flight attendants always tell you to place an oxygen mask over your own nose and face *before* you help the person sitting next to you. The same is true in corporate America. Despite the disappointments, various stresses, and long work hours, you owe it to yourself and your employees to make sure you are in the best physical condition possible. That means exercise, a healthy diet, and time to decompress and relax.

Timothy S. Taylor

Former Senior Counsel of the New York State United Teachers Union

"As long as I have my health and my happiness I don't care if I have $75 or $75 million, because all the money in the world is not going to bring you happiness or restore your health. Or buy you another precious minute of life. Live your life, be happy, strive to make a positive influence in people's lives, but don't let people steal your joy. You're gonna need that joy."

It has never been easy to be an executive of color. If you reach this point in your career, it is more than likely that you have perfected the ability of making White colleagues and co-workers feel comfortable. You are a *safe person of color*. Over the years, you've been rewarded with promotions, salary increases, elevated titles, and more responsibilities for making those Whites around you feel comfortable. Indeed, their comfort becomes your currency.

It is not easy to escape from the external validation of pleasing others to the detriment of yourself. External validation from your

P.S. Perkins

*Human Communication
Practitioner;
Author of* The Art and Science of
Communication

"Code-switching is a necessity
that I have mastered.
Everybody has an accent.
Everybody has a dialect.
Everybody code-switches:
women code-switch, you
code-switch, I code-switch.
We all do. Unless you hold the
power and you control the
game pieces. Very few people
have that ability or have that
opportunity. So do I code-
switch? Of course, I do. I'm
doing it with you right now."

White peers can become as addictive as an opioid. You will probably code-switch and act rather than being your true authentic self. If this persists for a long while, you may even forget who you actually are. Of course, you enjoy hearing your peers congratulating you for a job well done. But you must make sure that their compliments do not come at the sacrifice of being your authentic self. We have all done this to move up in corporate America. It's important to be conscious of this so you do not lose yourself. Your self-worth is paramount—and surely exists beyond the validation of others in the workplace. At times, I have lost myself and my identity in trying to please others. It's a feeling of being lost at sea, unsure of which way to travel to get back to shore. It's hard to recover your bearings and make it back. Remember to always stay grounded in who you are and your purpose.

CHAPTER 14

Adapt to the Workforce of the Future

The Rules for Navigating Through a Post-Pandemic Business Environment

In order to grow we must be open to new ideas . . . new ways of
doing things . . . new ways of thinking.

*—George Raveling, former college basketball player and coach.
Received the original copy of the "I Have A Dream" Speech
from MLK after the March on Washington in 1963*

As America climbs out of the Coronavirus Pandemic and we slowly
adjust to some semblance of normalcy, the question remains, what
will become of the workplace we once knew? Economists continue to
warn us of the *great resignation*, which purports that close to 80% of all
employed job seekers believe they can make more money by
changing jobs.[1]

As inflation continues to rise and reach levels of 8% or higher,
annual pay raises of 3%–4% will be insufficient. This is only further
motivation for workers to find new jobs with higher salaries to make
up for the decreased buying power of their current incomes since the
onset of the pandemic.

Additionally, after working remotely for three-plus years,
America's corporate workforce has had a glimpse of what life can be
like. One survey from Joblists.com found that 61% of all job seekers
are interested in remote job opportunities, while 45% say they will
quit their jobs if they are forced to return back to the office in person.[2]
However, the pandemic-riddled economy has not hit everyone the
same. The data are clear: American workers of color are once again
being left behind. All races saw unemployment decline as COVID-19
subsided. But according to a recent study from the Brookings
Institution, while the overall unemployment rate for the United States
lowered to 3.9%, Latino/Hispanic rates declined to 4.9%. Black
American rates *increased* from 6.5% to 7.1% while the rate for every
other ethnicity declined![3]

What is so confounding about these statistics is the fact that
although more Black Americans are entering the workforce and seeking employment than ever, the more they are being passed over for
advanced jobs. Despite the greatest demand for workers in America's
recent history, the unemployment rates for people of color remain

high even after the federal aid and pandemic stimulus funds have been exhausted.

When educational attainment is added into the equation, the numbers do not improve. White unemployment rates for workers without a high school diploma are the same as Black unemployment rates for workers with one! Additionally, Blacks and Native Americans with a bachelor's degree or higher have steeper unemployment rates than their peers with the same degree.

One of the many explanations for these disparities is the recent COVID-19 vaccination rates. On average, Black Americans are less likely to be vaccinated than other races and ethnicities.[4] This stems from years of distrust in the American healthcare system. The outcomes have resulted in numerous Black Americans being excluded from this post-pandemic economy based on their vaccination status.

All of these data points lead to a bleak outlook for racial equity in the workplace for people of color. Additionally, the plight of Black female professionals is an important call to action. As you know by now, Black women are severely underrepresented in leadership roles. W. E. B. Du Bois said it best: "But what of Black women? . . . I most sincerely doubt if any other race of women could have brought its fineness up through so devilish a fire."[6] Only 1.4% of Black women occupy C-Suite roles at present.[6] Black and Hispanic/Latina women are less likely to draw support from their managers or have access to senior leaders. They face more microaggressions and feel increased pressure to perform.

As an executive of color, if you are in a position to give a voice to the voiceless, it is your imperative to improve these bleak statistics. Never let your presence as an executive of color delude you into thinking diversity has been accomplished. As we return to work and embrace the aftermath of the great resignation, we will need to adapt to the differences we see in the workplace. How we communicate, hold meetings, network with peers and senior leaders, and navigate corporate politics will all be different post-pandemic. Success will be dependent on adjusting to this change.

Toyin Ajayi

Co-Founder and CEO of Cityblock Health, a healthcare start-up valued at $5.7 billion focused on improving the health of underserved urban communities

"I am a Black woman in a very conspicuous leadership role doing work on behalf of marginalized people, including, but not exclusively, people of color. I have that feeling that I cannot afford to fail us because a failure on my part would provide ammunition to so many other people with a belief structure about what people like me are capable of. That's an added layer of pressure that I don't think White male executives experience. I do I think about that. I can't afford to fail for us because it will have impact far beyond my team, my patients, and me. It will have implications for people I've never even met who look like me and are trying to establish themselves as leaders. That added layer of responsibility is certainly something that we carry."

Many companies are opting for hybrid models where employees come to the office two to three days a week, which makes it more difficult to build a rapport with your colleagues. There are fewer opportunities to socialize with co-workers or even see them as you pass through the hallways between meetings. As such, if you are a new employee and have yet to meet people in the company other than those you work closely with, it is important to make sure you can meet key stakeholders throughout the company. The pre-pandemic way was with a cup of coffee or stopping by someone's desk. In the post-pandemic world, it happens through emails and Zoom chats.

Desmond was a new employee who started in my company one year into the pandemic. He was joining a small team of three, so his sphere of influence was quite small. He met his other teammates and a few other employees, but for the most part, he had limited exposure to other parts of the organization. After about six months into the role, Desmond decided to reach out to me through LinkedIn. His message was concise:

Dear Errol.

It was a pleasure meeting you. I am a recent new hire and had the opportunity to hear you speak in a meeting a few weeks ago. It was a pleasant surprise to learn you also went to NYU. If your schedule allows, I'd love to learn more about the company and see if I can be of assistance to you in any way.

Desmond

The note was short and sweet. It clearly stated some basic information. Most importantly, it had a firm ask, and he got to the point succinctly. By using LinkedIn, Desmond did not use a formal work email to introduce himself. This is key because I would receive the message at my leisure rather than seeing the note during work hours. He found something in common with me, which helped to build the first basis for our rapport. Finding commonalities with people you're networking is a brilliant way to connect with them. I soon reached out to Desmond and suggested a Zoom call for us to speak. Upon meeting, we had a great conversation for 30 minutes. I was able to answer some of his questions about our company's strategy and focus areas. I also agreed to introduce him to some other individuals who could better answer some of his questions and, perhaps, eventually help him in his career.

This type of networking is common in the office setting. Desmond might have met me in an elevator or even decided to come to my office and walk by in an attempt to gain my attention. However, now that the future of work looks different, networking will too. It's important to hone your networking or bonding skills to make sure you can build your own personal board of directors within your firm. As discussed earlier in the book, your personal board of directors are the few people you have hand-selected who can provide guidance and direction as you pursue your career aspirations.

Given the nonstop busyness of work, many executives may easily default to "out of sight, out of mind." That is, if they do not actively see you on Zoom calls or in their inbox, they forget you exist. It is your job to stay relevant to your peers, your leaders, and your personal board of directors so that they stay engaged in your career development.

LESSON 14.1: SEEK OUT FACE TIME

If you're in middle management, or one or two levels away from the head of your division, it never hurts to get face time with that division leader. When everyone was in the office four to five days a week, this was much easier to do. I remember getting to the office early or leaving late and having those moments with my division heads when they passed by my cubicle. Those interactions were priceless. It's also effective to have a rapport with your boss's boss (or in some cases, your boss's boss's boss). They should know you directly as an individual, as opposed to only hearing about you and your value through someone else's lens. But you must be careful with these matters. You should be fully transparent with your direct supervisor if you go over their head, especially if you intend on sharing information unbeknownst to your direct supervisor.

Once again, building a similar rapport in a remote setting is much harder and will require a bit more strategy. One strategy is proposing to your supervisor 30-minute meetings with the division head or their boss, whichever makes more sense, for purposes of career development conversations. These meetings can be quarterly if you are a lower-level employee or every month or every six weeks if you are higher up the totem pole. Frequency can be a discussion topic with your supervisor.

The goal of these interactions is to learn from the division lead and ask probing questions about the company's mission and vision over the next few years. In the process, you can seek guidance on your own career. Since access to your leaders is no longer left up to chance in the office, interactions now must planned thoughtfully. If there is pushback from your supervisor on such an idea, try to lower the frequency of such meetings to twice a year. Think about proposing this idea if you ever have any interactions with your division head. If they say yes, inform your supervisor about the conversation and seek their guidance on how to follow through.

These types of meetings are called *Skip-Level meetings*. I recall when I had them with my CEO while reporting to the head of my division. For transparency, I would always disclose to my division head the parts of the conversation with my CEO that dealt with relevant work. This infused trust in the relationship between my division head and me and allowed my relationship with my CEO to prosper.

Skip-Level meetings are a great way to build relationships with leaders you typically do not have access to. It also enables you to gain valuable insights about the direction of the company. More context into *why* the company is doing something always helps *what* you are doing day-to-day. Also, it's useful to tie your daily activities to the company's mission overall. Use the time with your division head wisely. A good or bad meeting can very well determine if there will be future ones. Make sure you come prepared with a proposed agenda, questions, and a game plan for the overall relationship.

LESSON 14.2: LEVERAGE PRIVATE CHAT

Pre-pandemic, everyone was taught to have an "elevator pitch." These are the words you'd say if you happened to be in the elevator with the CEO and he or she asked you how things were going. In a post-pandemic world of virtual meetings and hybrid office schedules, these spontaneous meetings are rare. You will have to leverage all the tools at your disposal. Using great tact and discernment, a video teleconference can be an optimal opportunity to chat with one of the leaders in the company if your message pertains to the topic at hand. For example, once a month, I join an all-employee sales division virtual Zoom call. I enjoy seeing the entire team and catching up with them. At the beginning of the meeting, I provide some corporate updates for 5–10 minutes before handing the meeting back over to their Vice President.

After my remarks, one of the directors sent me a private message to thank me for sharing the business updates. He also asked a very thoughtful follow-up question about our implementation risk for one of the topics I discussed. I was impressed by the question and proceeded to correspond with the director through private messages on Zoom. As we ended the conversation, I invited him to arrange some time with me over the next few weeks to further discuss the topic.

This was an excellent use of the Zoom private chat function to have an impromptu skip-level conversation. It takes guts and judgment to know when to take advantage of such an opportunity. Most video conferencing applications like Zoom, Microsoft Teams, Google Meet, and WebEx all have private messaging options. The important thing is to use this function properly. The wrong message can hinder a relationship just as much as the right message can enhance one.

> *Pro Tip: It's important to make sure you properly private message someone and not send your message to the whole group on the call! The same obviously goes for email messages.*

LESSON 14.3: ENHANCE YOUR EMOTIONAL INTELLIGENCE (EQ)

Emotional intelligence was always a required skill before the pandemic. It is now an absolutely necessity in our virtual work environment. The proverbial reading of the room is that much harder when done through a computer screen with multiple faces staring at you from their Zoom boxes. It's harder to assess tone and understand posture. All the nonverbal intangibles of human communication are greatly diminished when seen through a computer screen. That was the invaluable benefit of meeting in person pre-pandemic. Face-to-face, you can tell by a glance across the table how someone may be feeling. Employees with high emotional intelligence are not only aware of their own emotions and facial expressions when listening to someone—they are also that much more attuned to everyone else's. There is the timeless cliché that actions speak louder than words. And they most certainly do! As do facial expressions. Can you perceive these expressions in your peers and senior leaders? Even the small subtle ones? Do you even try?

When I join a Zoom meeting, I always make it a point to scroll through all the pages of people to see who is present and whether their camera is on or off. You can pick up subtle cues in Zoom if someone unmutes, for example, as it intimates they may speak or have a desire to. You can visibly see when someone is texting on their phone or focused on something else on their screen other than the meeting at hand. Since it is harder to see someone's mannerisms, there are other hints to pick up on like tone and voice volume. Lean in to enhancing your emotional intelligence. A strong skill set in this area can mean the difference between being on the fast track for a promotion or not. The better you can access a room, the greater your communication skills will be. Strong communication skills galvanize confidence in your work.

LESSON 14.4: LEARN TO PIVOT

Pivoting is the ability to effortlessly switch topics during a presentation based on the questions and discussion in the room. It is such an important skill for success in a virtual world. Pivoting during a conversation takes confidence and preparation. The ability to pivot is more than just rehearsing your PowerPoint slides. It means you have developed a deep and intimate knowledge of your business, which leads to authentically answering questions with confidence.

If you're in a meeting and questions are generated on your first few slides that are scheduled to be answered later in the presentation, pivoting means you will advance the slides to that section to answer the questions posed. This requires EQ, deep knowledge of the topic at hand, and nimbleness to engage in a real-time conversation. Sometimes your answers will not be in the prepared materials. Having the ability to pivot to the important questions can lead to a very rich discussion with strong participation from your stakeholders.

Pivoting can lead to questions for which you lack the answers. Have the confidence to say, "That's a great question. Let me look into that and get back to you." Refrain from nonanswer answers, which is when you do not know the answer and you provide the facts and figures you do know to sound knowledgeable, while leaving the original question unanswered. No one likes it when politicians nonanswer questions. Please don't pick up this habit. Answering questions directly exudes confidence. Being transparent when not knowing an answer exudes integrity. Answering a question off-topic via a successful pivot exudes agility. If you can utilize all three, you are poised for success.

LESSON 14.5: LIGHTS, CAMERA, ACTION

Navigating virtual meetings takes some intentionality. I bought a ring light for my Zoom meetings so that my face would be visible on camera during meetings. I also have a microphone to ensure that my sound is crisp and professional. These are easy actions that can be taken to improve how you come across.

Additionally, a camera that is always off can be interpreted as a lack of engagement in the conversation. If you are the only one in the Zoom room with your camera off, think about whether you want to be such an outlier. Are you in a meeting with important clients? Just understand that the camera being off can send a disrespectful message, particularly if you are the only one with it off. Of course, if there are valid reasons for the camera being off, then it can be excused. But if these reasons are not shared with the group, no one will know. You are leaving it up to the assumptions of your audience. I am a firm believer in controlling your own message, especially as a person of color. A simple message at the beginning of the Zoom call or teleconference can go a long way.

"Happy to be on the call. Just a heads up—I'll have my camera off for this meeting, but I am actively listening."

Or

"You know, the kids are home from school today. Camera is off, but I am present."

I also strongly believe that there is also an unspoken dress code for virtual meetings. When the pandemic first hit, I recall still dressing up in a full professional outfit while working from home. It initially felt awkward to be at home in front of a computer screen. The only element of familiarity I had were the work clothes I wore. After a few weeks, I slowly morphed into wearing basketball shorts on the bottom, a buttoned-up dress shirt on the top. I believe the cost of dressing down is higher for a person of color than it is for others. As a younger executive, my goal was to convey maturity rather than youthfulness. It goes without saying that the clothes you wear on a Zoom call can impact how your colleagues think about you. It can also lead to negative racial stereotypes about your work ethic or your perceived value.

In 1998, Anthony Greenwald, Debbie McGhee, and Jordan Schwartz published a seminal paper in the *Journal of Personality and Social Psychology* called "Measuring Individual Differences in Implicit Cognition: The Implicit Association Test."[7] In it, Greenwald and his team state that our brain makes associations between people and things, and those associations can influence our attitudes and actions toward them without our even knowing.

Thus, the Implicit Association Test (IAT) was born. The test involves subjects having to categorize two different concepts with an attribute. For example, the researchers tested flowers and insects with the words *pleasant* and *unpleasant*. The people in the study naturally paired flowers with pleasant and insects with unpleasant. This showed an implicit positive bias toward flowers as compared to insects.

The study also did the same for Black and White people using the same words: pleasant and unpleasant. To the degree you are more inclined to assign unpleasant attributes to pictures of Black people, the more likely it is that you have a negative bias toward them. Researchers were now able to measure this implicit bias on a spectrum. The IAT is considered one of the most influential psychological developments over the past 30 years. The conclusion from this groundbreaking research is that negative biases are real. Rather than living in denial, we have to learn to accept this reality and formulate strategies, processes, and tactics to uncover and reduce these biases.

This all starts with transparency. When a company completes its annual performance reviews, it should take the time to understand trends. Were a disproportionate number of lower ratings allocated to a specific race, gender, ethnic group, or underrepresented employees? If so, was this by chance? Can the results be validated with an extra set of eyes? The one benefit of Zoom is that you can look around the room in a more organized fashion and take stock of your surroundings. An exercise everyone should do is to scan the meetings they attend for just one week to see how much they reflect the overall diversity of the company. It's a helpful check to ensure that inclusion and equity continue to be a focus.

LESSON 14.6: PARTICIPATE IN DE&I INITIATIVES

Another great way to ensure that you are properly networking within your company in a post-pandemic world is to participate in more DE&I initiatives. If not you, then who? While in-person meetings remain scarce and opportunities for meeting new people are few and far between, one way to enhance your visibility is by joining an Employee Resource Group (ERG) at your company. These groups serve as affinity groups of like-minded employees seeking to build community and contribute to the personal and professional growth of all. A recent *Forbes* article found that 90% of Fortune 500 companies currently have ERGs.[8] Not all ERGs are created equal. Please make sure you are joining a group that is both active and impactful in your organization. While they are not the panacea for workplace diversity, ERGs are one of several tools that can be used to develop leadership skills, foster inclusion, brand yourself, and enhance your exposure to senior leaders of the company.

Back in 2006, I created an ERG at one of the largest health insurance companies in the country. At the time, I was a member of the diversity council when the Chief Diversity Officer first implemented ERGs at our company. I was immediately intrigued. To obtain approval, each ERG had to submit a business plan, find an executive sponsor within the company who would support the initiative, and secure at least 20 employees who would participate.

My co-chair and I immediately got to work. We were both young professionals seeking opportunities for mentorship, career growth, exposure, and access. Those became the pillars of our ERG that we formed from scratch. We also landed an executive sponsor who at the time was the youngest executive in the company reporting to the CEO. The sheer fact that she was our sponsor meant we had immediate access to power. This paid off in droves. Many of our entry-level employees did not have a forum to meet other colleagues. In fact, many co-workers on the same team met through our forums rather than through work interactions.

Our group was, in a sense, tearing down the walls. We were a massive company; however, our ERG made the company feel that much smaller. Our network of people working in different states, departments, and business segments grew exponentially. These connections also helped me do my job more efficiently.

I was able to leverage my ERG connections to open doors to even more possibilities. We were all willing to help our ERG colleagues in their work while we collaborated on our personal and professional growth. We even held social events and meetups in each state by establishing site chairs who would assist with onboarding new members and coordinating activities. When I traveled to different offices in different cities, I would always make sure to stop by and meet my fellow ERG members. I know many colleagues who obtained job promotions through their ERG connections, which was precisely one of the goals we had when we started the group.

Within two years we were one of the largest ERGs in the company. Leading a company-sanctioned group with well over 100 members also gave me legitimate leadership experience while I was in an individual contributor role. Of course, the exposure also helped boost my career. At the time, our marketing team was looking for creative ways to market high-deductible health plans to younger populations. Our ERG was specifically solicited to provide candid feedback on their campaigns. We also spearheaded many mentoring programs within the company. Leading this ERG also brought me closer to my Chief Diversity Officer, the leadership team in my state, and other executives around the company. Indeed, I credit my advancement in the company to the exposure and access I received leading an ERG.

If you are fortunate enough to have an active ERG at your company, it's a good idea to get involved. In a more virtual world, ERGs are becoming one of the only options to attain exposure to senior leaders and your colleagues. As you know by now, there has been a resurgence and a refocus on DE&I programs in our country. A LinkedIn analysis found that senior-level diversity roles have grown by 107% over the past five years. In 2020, there was a growth of more than 400% in diversity roles, right after the murder of George Floyd and nationwide protests revolving around social justice.[9] This renewed focus is yet another reason to join ERGs.

CHAPTER 15

Lead While Leaving a Legacy

Make the Greatest Impact You Possibly Can

Now is the accepted time, not tomorrow, not some more convenient season. It is today that our best work can be done and not some future day or future year.
—*William Edward Burghardt Du Bois, Civil Rights Pioneer, Author, and Historian, and Co-Founder of the NAACP*

Undoubtedly, when you find the way up to a corner office in corporate America, whether physically or virtually, you will take a step back and realize how many hands helped you get there. Climbing to the top of your corporate mountain will just be the beginning. Now that you are at the top and see the world more clearly, you can turn your focus toward leading your teams while leaving a legacy.

One of the hardest hypothetical questions you can ever be asked is: *What do you want written on your tombstone?* A similar question can be asked with regard to your role as an executive of color at your company: *When you leave your firm, how do you want to be remembered?* It's a hard question to answer, but you should give it some thought so you can be intentional about where and how you spend your time.

Think through the programs you can create or promote that will leave the company better than the way you found it. Consider your biggest hurdles and difficulties you faced and what changes can be made to have a smoother journey up the mountain for future employees of color. Strive to focus on tangible ways to increase diversity, expand equity, and prioritize inclusion.

Rudine Sims Bishop, considered the mother of multicultural children's literature, speaks eloquently about how books can serve as windows, mirrors, and sliding doors for children. Windows because a child can get a glimpse into a new world, one they have not previously seen by learning from the experiences of others. Mirrors because a child can see themselves in a book, which can lead to a boost in their self-esteem from the affirmation of their culture. Sliding doors because some books allow children to enter the story and fully immerse themselves in the lives of the characters.[1]

This same analogy can be used in corporate America. As an executive of color, you have the opportunity to perform all three roles for your teams, your peers on the executive team, and for society as a whole. You can be a window for employees of different races and ethnicities to grasp how you navigate the political minefield of a corporation or organization. You may be one of the few executives of color they have ever seen or worked with. Thus, your impression can hold weight and be meaningful to your organization. The image of an executive of color can be a blank slate to many. All your actions have an outsized impact on how that picture gets painted.

You can also be a mirror to the many employees of color looking to grow their careers by seeking insights, advice, and support. Be ever present and realize your community is always watching you. They watch whether you say good morning to the janitor or if you treat the administrative staff with dignity and respect. They witness whether you are authentic and vulnerable. Just thriving in the company gives people hope to continuously strive for excellence.

Some of you will be a sliding door. This is a very close bond you will build with a few employees of color who will be able to see and know the real you. These will be your mentees and the people you will champion within the company. These close relationships may last a lifetime. I know the sliding doors in my life, and today I am lucky enough to call them my friends as well.

Connecting to the employees in our company is our charge. It becomes our life's work. With so many people of color at the lower levels of many companies and so few at the top, make sure to lead while leaving a legacy, and plant the seeds for the future growth of diversity. If you have the honor and privilege to leave such a legacy, take this opportunity seriously. There is no higher honor than leaving a place better than the way you found it. The climb up the mountain will not be easy, but we are fortunate to

Lucy M. Lopez

General Counsel and Chief Legal Officer at Spencer Stuart, a leading global executive search and leadership advisory firm

"I would like to look back on my career and know that I have created opportunities for others in the workplace; that while solving for problems in the corporate world, I also enabled the professional development and growth of those I work with, the next generation of leaders."

live in a time where corporations are focused on this important work. Let's harness this moment.

During my 18 years in corporate America, I have done my best to create programs in an effort to leave a legacy. In all humility, I have described several examples below, but brainstorm some for yourself and set the world on fire.

- Hired, promoted, and recruited over 300 employees of color as a people leader at various firms.

- Wrote numerous letters of recommendation for employees of color seeking higher education.

- Served as a mentor, speaker, and advisor to Fordham under-graduate students of color as a member of the President's Club and the Athletics Advisory Committee.

- Served on several nonprofit boards focused on helping vulnerable populations in America and abroad.

- Created an Employee Resource Group called HYPE at one of the largest health insurance companies in the country.

- Created a paid college degree program for employees who sought to move into senior management positions.

- Formed a Council of Employees of Color with direct access to the executive team.

- Became a founding member of a Fortune 50 company's Diversity Committee.

- Developed a strategy for a nonprofit foundation focused on vulnerable populations.

- Led DE&I efforts at multiple companies.

LESSON 15: DARE TO DREAM BIG

The last lesson of the book is easy but audacious. Your dreams should be big enough that you feel a little unsteady about achieving them. Those butterflies in your stomach that form when you think about a dream is a sign that the dream is big enough to pursue. Chase your butterflies! The world is changing, the demographics of the United States are shifting, and more employees of color are finding themselves in leadership positions. Now is the perfect time to dream big and change the world. The lives of many who look like you and me are depending on it. We are all waiting for your success. I'm still climbing my mountain and learning on the way up. Hopefully we will reach the top together.

INTERVIEWS

Interviews with executives of color include (in alphabetical order):

- Dr. Toyin Ajayi—Co-Founder and CEO of Cityblock Health, a healthcare start-up valued at $5.7 billion focused on improving the health of underserved urban communities

- Pauline Bent—Vice President, Private Bank; former Vice President at Goldman Sachs, J.P. Morgan, and Pershing

- Denise J. Brown—Entertainment attorney and consultant; NYU professor; former Senior Vice President of Warner Bros. Records; ordained minister

- Robert Childs—Executive Vice President, Office of Enterprise Inclusion, Diversity and Business Engagement, American Express

- Stanley E. Grayson—Board Member of TD Bank, N.A., and Mutual of America Investment Corporation; former Vice Chairman and COO of M. R. Beal and Company, the nation's oldest and continuously operated minority-owned investment bank; former Deputy Mayor for Finance and Economic Development, New York City

- Rashidi Hendrix—Owner, Producer, and Manager of Metallic Entertainment, a film, TV, and music production

- Indira Hector—Global HR Leader, AstraZeneca; former global HR Director, Bristol Myers Squibb

- Bruce Jackson—Associate General Counsel and Managing Director, Strategic Partnership, Microsoft; Author of *Never Far from Home*

- Sachin H. Jain, MD, MBA—President and CEO of SCAN Group and Health Plan; Adjunct Professor of Medicine,

Stanford University School of Medicine; contributor at *Forbes*; recognized by *Modern Healthcare* magazine as one of American healthcare's 100 most influential leaders

- Lucy M. Lopez—General Counsel and Chief Legal Officer at Spencer Stuart, a leading global executive search and leadership advisory firm; Former Deputy General Counsel for McKinsey & Company, Inc.

- P.S. Perkins—Human Communication Practitioner; diversity and inclusion specialist; Author of *The Art and Science of Communication*

- Kate Simpson (pseudonym) —Client Account Manager, Big Five accounting firm

- Timothy S. Taylor, Esq.—Renowned Arbitrator and Mediator; Former Senior Counsel of the New York State United Teachers Union; former Assistant Professor of Law at The Sage Colleges

NOTES

PREFACE

1. Nicholas Jones, Rachel Marks, Roberto Ramirez, and Merarys Rios-Vargas, "2020 Census Illuminates Racial and Ethnic Composition of the Country," United States Census Bureau, August 12, 2021.
2. Jessica Guynn and Brent Schrotenboer, "Why Are There Still So Few Black Executives in America?," *USA Today*, August 20, 2020.
3. Jeanne Sahadi, "After Years of Talking About Diversity, the Number of Black Leaders at US Companies Is Still Dismal," *CNN*, June 2, 2020.
4. Khristopher Brooks, "Why So Many Black Business Professionals Are Missing from the C-Suite," CBS News, December 10, 2019.
5. Ruth Umoh, "The Dearth of Black CEOs: How Corporate Diversity Initiatives Ignore People of Color," *Forbes*, December 10, 2019.
6. Emma Hinchliffe, "Women Run 37 Fortune 500 Companies, a Record High," *Fortune*, May 18, 2020.
7. Jones et al., "2020 Census Illuminates Racial and Ethnic Composition."
8. J. Yo-Jud Cheng, Boris Groysberg, and Paul M. Healy, "Why Do Boards Have So Few Black Directors?" *Harvard Business Review*, August 13, 2020.
9. Kosmas Papadopoulos, "U.S. Board Diversity Trends in 2019," *ISS Analytics*, May 31, 2019.
10. Spencer Stuart, "2021 S&P 500 Board Diversity Snapshot," July 2021, https://www.spencerstuart.com/research-and-insight/2021-sp-500-board-diversity-snapshot.
11. Peter Eavis, "Board Diversity Increased in 2021. Some Ask What Took So Long," *New York Times*, January 3, 2022.
12. Guynn and Schrotenboer, "Why Are There Still So Few Black Executives?".
13. American Psychological Association, "Racial and Ethnic Identity," *APA Style*, September 2019, https://apastyle.apa.org/style-grammar-guidelines/bias-free-language/racial-ethnic-minorities.

CHAPTER 2: EMBRACE YOUR DEFINING MOMENTS

1. Yale Law School, Lillian Goldman Law Library, "The Articles of Confederation," March 1, 1781.

2. U.S. Customs and Border Protection, "1891: Immigration Inspection Expands," January 4, 2022.

3. Anna Diamond, "The 1924 Law That Slammed the Door on Immigrants and the Politicians Who Pushed it Back Open," *Smithsonian Magazine*, May 19, 2020, https://www.smithsonianmag.com/history/1924-law-slammed-door-immigrants-and-politicians-who-pushed-it-back-open-180974910/.

4. Abby Budiman, "Key Findings about U.S. Immigrants," Pew Research, August 20, 2020.

5. Ed Young, "A Tissue Sample from 1966 Held Traces of Early HIV," *The Atlantic*, August 16, 2019.

6. George Annas, "Detention of HIV-Positive Haitians at Guantanamo—Human Rights and Medical Care," *New England Journal of Medicine*, August 19, 1993.

7. Bruce Lampert, "Now, No Haitians Can Donate Blood," *New York Times*, March 14, 1990.

8. Tom Reiss, *The Black Count: Glory, Revolution, Betrayal, and the Real Count of Monte Cristo* (New York: Broadway Paperbacks, 2016), 7.

9. Annalisa Quinn, "Chinua Achebe and the Bravery of Lions," *NPR*, March 22, 2013.

10. Caroline Janney, "United Daughters of the Confederacy," *Encyclopedia Virginia*, Virginia Humanities, July 26, 2021.

11. "Haiti Country Profile," BBC, July 7, 2021.

12. Errol Pierre (executive producer), *1804: The Hidden History of Haiti*, directed by Tariq Nasheed (Los Angeles: King Flex Entertainment, 2017), https://www.imdb.com/name/nm9343465/?ref_=ttfc_fc_cr24.

13. "Jean-Michel Basquiat," Embassy of the Republic of Haiti, n.d., accessed May 18, 2022, https://www.haiti.org/dt_team/jean-michel-basquiat/.

14. Robin Pogrebin and Scott Reyburn, "A Basquiat Sells for 'Mind-Blowing' $110.5 Million at Auction," *New York Times*, May 18, 2017.

CHAPTER 3: RECLAIM YOUR SEAT

1. Victoria Medvec, Scott Madey, and Thomas Gilovich, "When Less Is More: Counterfactual Thinking and Satisfaction Among Olympic Medalists," *Journal of Personality and Social Psychology*, 69, no. 4 (November 1995): 603–610.

2. For more, see Christian Jarrett, "Feeling Like a Fraud," *British Psychological Society* 23 (May 2010): 380–383, https://thepsychologist.bps.org.uk/volume-23/edition-5/feeling-fraud; Pauline Rose Clance, *The Impostor*

Phenomenon: Overcoming the Fear That Haunts Your Success (Atlanta: Peach Tree, 1985); Bridgette J. Peteet, LaTrice Montgomery, and Jerren C. Weekes, "Predictors of Imposter Phenomenon among Talented Ethnic Undergraduate Students," *Journal of Negro Education* 84, no. 2 (Spring 2015): 175–186, https://doi.org/10.7709/jnegroeducation.84.2.0175.

3. Cassi Pittman Claytor, *Black Privilege: Modern Middle-Class Blacks With Credentials and Cast To Spend* (Stanford, CA: Stanford University Press, 2020), 87.

4. Jomills Braddock and James McPartland, "How Minorities Continue to Be Excluded from Equal Employment Opportunities: Research on Labor Market and Institutional Barriers," *Journal of Social Issues*, 43, no. 1 (1987): 5–39.

5. Astrid Groenewegen, "Kahneman Fast and Slow Thinking Explained," SUE Behavioural Design, n.d., https://suebehaviouraldesign.com/kahneman-fast-slow-thinking/ (accessed May 18, 2022). See also Daniel Kahneman, *Thinking, Fast and Slow* (New York: Farrar, Straus and Giroux, 2015).

6. Jenny Guidi, Marcella Lucente, Nicoletta Sonino, and Giovanni A. Fava, "Allostatic Load and Its Impact on Health: A Systematic Review," *Psychotherapy and Psychosomatics* 90 (2021): 11–27.

CHAPTER 4: HARNESS YOUR DISTINCTIONS

1. New York State Association of Criminal Defense Lawyers and National Association of Criminal Defense Lawyers, "The New York State Trial Penalty: The Constitutional Right to Trial Under Attack," 2021 https://www.nacdl.org/Document/NewYorkStateTrialPenaltyRighttoTrialUnderAttack.

2. New York Civil Liberties Union, "Stop-and-Frisk in the de Blasio Era," March 2019, https://www.nyclu.org/en/publications/stop-and-frisk-de-blasio-era-2019.

3. "Stop-and-Frisk Data," New York Civil Liberties Union, n.d., https://www.nyclu.org/en/stop-and-frisk-data (accessed May 27, 2022); U.S. Census Bureau, "General Demographics Characteristics," *2005 American Community Survey (ACS), New York City*, https://www1.nyc.gov/assets/planning/download/pdf/data-maps/nyc-population/acs/acs_demo_05.pdf.

4. New York Civil Liberties Union, "Stop-and-Frisk in the de Blasio Era," March 2019, https://www.nyclu.org/en/publications/stop-and-frisk-de-blasio-era-2019.

5. Tori DeAngelis, "Unmasking 'Racial Micro Aggressions,'" *Monitor on Psychology* 40, no. 2 (February 2009): 42, https://www.apa.org/monitor/2009/02/microaggression.

6. Jeff Miller, "Harvard's Chester Pierce Was Trailblazer in His Field and on the Field," *Andscape*, September 29, 2016, https://andscape.com/features/harvards-chester-pierce-was-trailblazer-in-his-field-and-on-the-field/.

7. Monnica Williams, "Microaggressions: Clarification, Evidence, and Impact," *Perspectives on Psychological Science* 15, no. 1 (August 2019): 3–26, https://doi.org/10.1177/1745691619827499.

8. Sadia Corey and Daniel Garcia, "Black Lives Matter: Everywhere," *Savanta*, January 2021, https://savanta.com/view/how-do-black-employees-feel-in-the-workplace/.

9. Grace Donnelly, "Only 3% of Fortune 500 Companies Share Full Diversity Data," *Fortune*, July 7, 2017, https://fortune.com/2017/06/07/fortune-500-diversity/.

10. Vivian Hunt, Lareina Yee, Sara Prince, and Sundiatu Dixon-Fyle, "Delivery through diversity," McKinsey & Company, January 18, 2018, https://www.immigrationresearch.org/system/files/Delivering-through-diversity_full-report.compressed-min.pdf.

CHAPTER 7: RECOGNIZE AND HARNESS YOUR CHAMPIONS

1. "Mensch." Merriam-Webster.com Dictionary, https://www.merriam-webster.com/dictionary/mensch (accessed May 22, 2022).

2. Eugene Daniels, Krystal Campos, and Michael Cadenhead, "Richie Torres represents America's poorest congressional district. He's on a mission to save public housing," *Politico*, April 26, 2021, https://www.politico.com/news/2021/04/26/ritchie-torres-new-117th-congress-freshman-members-diversity-2021-484443.

3. Cindy Gallop and Tomas Chamorro-Premuzic, "7 Pieces of Bad Career Advice Women Should Ignore," *Harvard Business Review*, April 15, 2021, https://hbr.org/2021/04/7-pieces-of-bad-career-advice-women-should-ignore.

CHAPTER 8: OVERCOME THE ENTRY-LEVEL BLUES

1. W. E. B. Du Bois, "Strivings of the Negro People," *The Atlantic*, August 1897.

2. Courtney L. McCluney, Kathrina Robotham, Serenity Lee, Richard Smith, and Myles Durkee, "The Costs of Code-Switching," *Harvard*

Business Review, November 15, 2019, https://hbr.org/2019/11/the-costs-of-codeswitching.

3. Afran Ahmed, Tatyana Cruz, Aarushi Kaushal, Yusuke Kobuse, Kristen Wang, "Why Is There a Higher Rate of Impostor Syndrome among BIPOC?," *Across the Spectrum of Socioeconomics* 1, no. 2 (2020): 1–17, https://doi.org/10.5281/zenodo.4310477.

4. Kristi Dosh, "Golfers Make Better Business Executives," *Forbes*, May 16, 2016, https://www.forbes.com/sites/kristidosh/2016/05/16/golfers-make-better-business-executives/?sh=3c1f676db4a5.

5. Tsedale M. Melaku, Angie Beeman, David G. Smith, and W. Brad Johnson, "Be a Better Ally," *Harvard Business Review*, November–December 2020, https://hbr.org/2020/11/be-a-better-ally.

6. Sean Captain, "Workers Win Only 1% of Federal Civil Rights Lawsuits at Trial," *Fast Company*, July 31, 2017, https://www.fastcompany.com/40440310/employees-win-very-few-civil-rights-lawsuits.

CHAPTER 9: NAVIGATE AND SURVIVE BAD BOSSES

1. Sara Korolevich, "Horrible Bosses: Are American Workers Quitting Their Jobs or Quitting Their Managers?," *GoodHire*, January 11, 2022, https://www.goodhire.com/resources/articles/horrible-bosses-survey/.

2. U.S. Bureau of Labor Statistics, "Baby Boomers Born from 1957 to 1964 Held an Average of 12.3 Jobs from Ages 18 to 52," *Economics Daily*, August 27, 2019, https://www.bls.gov/opub/ted/2021/baby-boomers-born-from-1957-to-1964-held-an-average-of-12-4-jobs-from-ages-18-to-54.htm.

CHAPTER 10: GROW BY GIVING BACK

1. Kiran Dadi, "Leadership Is Action Not a Position," CastleBay Companies, August 27, 2020.

2. Fordham University, "About Donald McGannon," The McGannon Center.

3. World Radio History, "Most Independent Affiliate," *Sponsor Magazine*, June 29, 1957.

4. World Radio History, "Our Respects to Donald Henry McGannon," *Broadcasting/Telecasting*, November 21, 1955.

5. Obituary, "Donald McGannon, A Former Chairman of Broadcast Group," *New York Times*, May 24, 1984.

6. World Radio History, "Our Respects to Donald Henry McGannon," *Broadcasting/Telecasting*, November 21, 1955.

7. TimeMachine, "George Norford Is Named Vice President of Group W," *New York Times*, October 30, 1968.

8. Press Release, "National Urban League Honors Citi with 2007 Donald H McGannon Award," *Citi*, July 30, 2007.

9. Latin Dictionary, Latinitium, https://latinitium.com/latin-dictionaries/?t=lsn24756.

10. Poetry Foundation, "William Ernest Henley," https://www.poetryfoundation.org/poets/william-ernest-henley.

11. DOE Leadership and Offices, "Chancellor David C. Banks," NYC Department of Education.

CHAPTER 11: BE HONEST EVEN WHEN IT'S HARD

1. University of Southern Denmark (SDU), "The Emperor's New Clothes," H. C. Andersen Centre, September 19, 2019.

CHAPTER 12: LEAVE WITHOUT BURNING THE BRIDGE

1. David Ronayne, Daniel Sgroi, and Anthony Tuckwell, "How Susceptible Are You to the Sunk Cost Fallacy?," *Harvard Business Review*, July 15, 2021.

2. Devah Pager, Bart Bonikowski, and Bruce Western, "Discrimination in a Low-Wage Labor Market: A Field Experiment," *American Sociological Review* 74, no. 5 (October 2009): 777–799, https://doi.org/10.1177/000312240907400505.

3. Lincoln Quillian, Devah Pager, Ole Hexel, and Arnfinn H. Midtbøen, "Meta-analysis of Field Experiments Shows No Change in Racial discrimination in Hiring over Time," *PNAS* 114 (41): 10,870–10,875, September 12, 2017.

4. New York University, "Sherry Glied," *Our Faculty*.

5. Tony Lee, "The Pros and Cons of Counteroffers," SHRM, June 1, 2021.

CHAPTER 13: EXUDE EXECUTIVE PRESENCE

1. Bloomberg, "How Did I Get Here? Bernard Tyson," Bloomberg.com, 2015.

2. U.S. Securities and Exchange Commission, "Statement on Nasdaq's Diversity Proposals—A Positive First Step for Investors," SEC.gov, August 6, 2021.

3. Thomas Franck, "SEC Approves Nasdaq's Plan to Boost Diversity on Corporate Boards," CNBC, August 6, 2021, https://www.cnbc.com/2021/08/06/sec-approves-nasdaqs-plan-to-boost-diversity-on-corporate-boards.html.

4. Johnnie L. Cochran Jr. and Cyrus Mehri, "Black Coaches in the National Football League: Superior Performance, Inferior Opportunities," September 30, 2002, http://media.wix.com/ugd/520423_24cb6412ed275 8c7204b7864022ebb5d.pdf.

5. Ibid.

6. Associated Press, "Cochran Says Black Coaches Held to Different Standard," ESPN/NFL, October 2, 2002.

7. Bob Barnett, "Profile: Ray Kemp," Pro Football Hall of Fame, January 18, 2005.

8. Jim Trotter, "Trailblazing Steelers Scout Bill Nunn Deserves Spot in Hall of Fame," NFL, July 24, 2020.

9. Football Operations, "The Rooney Rule," NFL, https://operations.nfl.com/inside-football-ops/diversity-inclusion/the-rooney-rule/.

10. Douglas Wigdor, Michael Willemin, David Gottlieb, John Elefterakis, Nicholas Elefterakis, Raymond Panek, and John Atkinson, "Brian Flores, Steve Wilks, and Ray Horton, as Class Representatives, on behalf of themselves and all others similarly situated." United States District Court Southern District of New York, April 7, 2022.

11. Brooke Pryor, "Mike Tomlin, Convinced That 'You Can Use a Brian Flores on Your Staff,' Enthused to Add Pittsburgh Steelers' New Assistant Coach," ABC News, March 27, 2022.

12. Alliance for Board Diversity, "Missing Pieces Report: The Board Diversity Census of Women and Minorities on Fortune 500 Boards," 6th edition, Deloitte, 2020.

13. Ibid.

14. Laura Morgan Roberts, Anthony J. Mayo, and David A. Thomas, editors, *Race, Work, and Leadership: New Perspectives on the Black Experience* (Boston: Harvard Business Review Press, 2019); see also https://www.racework leadership.com/.

15. Karen Yuan, "Black Employees Say 'Performative Allyship' Is an Unchecked Problem in the Office," *Fortune*, June 19, 2020.

16. Bryan Walker and Sarah A. Soule, "Changing Company Culture Requires a Movement, Not a Mandate," *Harvard Business Review*, June 20, 2017.

CHAPTER 14: ADAPT TO THE WORKFORCE OF THE FUTURE

1. Joblist, "Joblist's U.S. Job Market Report: 2022 Trends," Joblist.com, January 6, 2022.
2. Ibid.
3. Kristen Brody and Anthony Barr, "December's Jobs Report Reveals a Growing Racial Employment Gap, Especially for Black Women," Brookings, January 11, 2022.
4. Nambi Ndugga, Latoya Hill, Samantha Artiga, and Sweta Haldar, "Latest Data on COVID-19 Vaccinations by Race/Ethnicity," KFF, April 7, 2022.
5. W. E. B. Du Bois Center, "Du Bois Quotes," The DuBois Papers, n.d., accessed May 27, 2022, http://duboiscenter.library.umass.edu/du-bois-quotes/.
6. Holly Corbett, "How to Be An Ally for Black Women in the Workplace," *Forbes*, February 22, 2022, https://www.forbes.com/sites/hollycorbett/2022/02/22/how-to-be-an-ally-for-black-women-in-the-workplace/?sh=60c0aa3b3123.
7. A. G. Greenwald, D. E. McGhee, and J. L. Schwartz, "Measuring Individual Differences in Implicit Cognition: The Implicit Association Test," *Journal of Personality and Social Psychology* 74, no. 6 (1998): 1464–1480.
8. Georgene Huang, "90% of Fortune 500 Companies Already Have a Solution to Gender Equality But Aren't Utilizing It," *Forbes*, November 13, 2017, https://www.forbes.com/sites/georgenehuang/2017/11/13/90-of-fortune-500-companies-already-have-a-solution-to-gender-equality-but-arent-utilizing-it/?sh=4a523c001c34.
9. Bruce Anderson, "Why the Head of Diversity Is the Job of the Moment," LinkedIn, September 2, 2020.

CHAPTER 15: LEAD WHILE LEAVING A LEGACY

1. Robin Chenoweth, "Rudine Sims Bishop: 'Mother' of Multicultural Children's Literature," OSU.edu, September 5, 2019.

ACKNOWLEDGMENTS

I would not be here without the help and support of so many in my tribe. I am particularly grateful to all those who see in me the things I cannot. First to my father: you are forever the consummate gentleman and the forever dreamer who has given me unconditional love and support from day one. To my mother: thank you for showing me the merits of hard work and education through the actions of your life. I watched and I listened.

Dan Pearson of D4 Entertainment heard my story. Jim Jermanok helped me bring it to life. Keith Wyche leaned in to help me get started. Yvonne Orji made me believe in the possibilities. David Banks inspired me. Ashley Michel gave me a safe space to be vulnerable and vent.

So many titans and captains of industry gave up their personal time and allowed me to interview them. A special thank you to Dr. Toyin Ajayi, Pauline Bent, Denise J. Brown, Robert Childs, Stan Grayson, Rashidi Hendrix, Indira Hector, Bruce Jackson, Dr. Sachin H. Jain, Lucy M. Lopez, P.S. Perkins, Kate Simpson, and Timothy S. Taylor.

Don Ashkenase, may you rest in peace. Thank you for being the giant in my corner. Pat Wang, your leadership is so influential and galvanizing. Thank you for leading by example and giving me a shot. Curtiss Jacobs, you have always had my back. I am forever indebted.

There are so many more people who helped along this journey who I have not named, but your fingerprints are woven into every single page of this book. You are my tribe, and I am indebted to you all. I will be thanking you and counting my blessings from now until my last days, and it still would not be enough. From the bottom of my heart, thank you again.

ABOUT THE AUTHORS

DR. ERROL L. PIERRE is a business executive, healthcare strategist, public speaker, professor, and author.

For the past 18 years, he has worked for both the largest for-profit and nonprofit health plans in New York, taught and given guest lectures at Ivy League institutions, and spoken in front of large crowds all over the world as a healthcare thought leader.

Errol earned his BS in Business Administration from Fordham University, his MPA in Health Policy and Financial Management from New York University, and his Doctorate in Business Administration (DBA) from the Zicklin School of Business at Baruch College. He currently teaches health economics as an adjunct professor at Columbia University, New York University, and Baruch College.

Errol also volunteers for various nonprofit organizations. He is a board member of the Arthur Ashe Institute for Urban Health, MediNova New York, and the One Hundred Black Men of Long Island. As a Fordham alum, he is a member of the President's Council and serves on the Athletic Advisory committee. Throughout his career, he has been recognized by several nonprofits and business organizations for his community service.

JIM JERMANOK is an award-winning writer, director, producer, author, and speaker based in New York. His words and photos can be seen in *The Washington Post*, *Indiewire*, *The Huffington Post*, and *The Boston Globe*. He has written two highly praised books: *Beyond The Craft: What You Need To Know To Make A Living Creatively!* and *Dive In! Real Estate Investment Advice From A Pro*. Jim wrote and produced the highly acclaimed romantic comedy *Passionada*, which was released by Columbia TriStar in over 150 countries. His film *Em* won the Grand

Jury Prize at the Seattle International Film Festival and the Criterion International Inspiration Award. He also created the global web series WWW.LIFEADVICE.TV in 2015. Jim is a former ICM agent who represented Arthur Miller, Shirley MacLaine, John Chancellor, Ben Kingsley, Dudley Moore, Helen Hayes, Alan Arkin, and General H. Norman Schwarzkopf, among others.

INDEX